TRANSFORMING ENCOUNTERS

Baptism, Assembly, and the Lord's Supper

JOHN MARK HICKS

REGNUM
MEDIA

TRANSFORMING ENCOUNTERS
Baptism, Assembly, and the Lord's Supper

Copyright © 2023 John Mark Hicks

Published by Regnum Media.

Regnum Media is the publishing imprint of the **Center for Christian Studies**
12407 N. Mopac Expy. Ste. 250-530
Austin TX 78758

www.christian-studies.org

CENTER FOR
CHRISTIAN STUDIES

Praise for
Transforming Encounters

As one who sat at the feet of Dr. Hicks during his teaching career, this book reminded me of many things I appreciated about his classes. *Transforming Encounters* is a study of Scripture that engages the trajectories of both testaments along with historical theology. Readers will be challenged to be better disciples when prompted to think about God's activity in the assembly, in baptism, and at the Lord's Table. Even as the contrast between "altar/table" or the definition of certain terms (sacrament, worship) might challenge some, this study serves as a gentle and helpful correction for those who have underestimated the blessing of our encounters with God.

> —**Doug Burleson**, PhD, Lectureship Director, Assistant Dean of College of Biblical Studies, Freed-Hardeman University, Henderson, Tennessee

Drawing on the author's expertise in historical theology, the Bible, and congregational life, this accessible manual invites disciples at all experience levels to deepen their understandings of fundamental moments of transformation and to enrich their practices in three key areas: the Christian assembly, baptism, and communion. With steady attention to the ways that God has revealed himself and shaped people in these encounters, and continues to do so, the book's structure, content, and study aids insightfully apply the material to the life of the disciple and the communal experience of the church.

> —**Jeff Childers**, DPhil, Professor of Biblical Studies, Graduate School of Theology; Director, Center for the Study of Ancient Religious Texts, Abilene Christian University, Abilene, Texas

Encountering the triune God. Proclaiming and experiencing the gospel. Committing to lives of authentic discipleship. For Hicks, this is what baptism, the worship assembly, and the Lord's Supper are all about. This is the kind of study that, combined with prayerful application, can deepen faith and transform the local church.

> —**Mark E. Powell**, PhD, Dean and Professor of Theology, Harding School of Theology, Memphis, Tennessee

After a lifetime of teaching, preaching, writing about, and practicing baptism, assembly, and the Lord's Supper, John Mark Hicks offers yet another gift to the church in this book. He skillfully explores these sacramental practices through Scripture's story of redemption—in the life of Israel, Jesus Christ, and the church. Biblical, approachable, and readable, this book is a call to return to the basics of church life, to elevate our understanding of these means of grace, and to expect a transformative encounter with the God who has called us into his eternal fellowship. Every Christian congregation and believer will benefit from this study.

—**Keith Stanglin,** PhD, Director, Center for Christian Studies, Austin, Texas; Professor of Historical Theology, Harding School of Theology, Memphis, Tennessee

Scripturally rich and pastorally insightful, this book provides accessible yet profound insights into baptism, the Lord's Supper, and church assembly as tangible means of grace in believers' lives. Its contents will intrigue those who were initially drawn to these practices as commands, yet want to understand their import beyond a transactional register; it will equally tantalize those who embrace these acts as sacramental mysteries of the faith, but long to press further into their biblical and practical significance. Best of all, Hicks' study of these "transforming encounters" offers an analogous opportunity to its readers, inviting us deeper into the story, love, and life of the Triune God.

—**Lauren Smelser White,** PhD, Assistant Professor of Theology, College of Bible and Ministry, Lipscomb University, Nashville, Tennessee

DEDICATION

I have been enriched by students throughout my
forty years of university teaching, and it is
to these women and men that
I dedicate this book.
Thank you!

Soli Deo Gloria

TABLE OF CONTENTS

DOCTRINA SERIES INTRODUCTION

Lesson Format

The Regnum Media *Doctrina* Series provides topical study on key doctrinal, ethical, and theological issues, and, as part of the broader mission of the Center for Christian Studies, seeks to make the best of relevant scholarship accessible to churches and individual Christians. This series is designed primarily with Bible class teachers in mind, but it is also intended for Christian readers who seek to grow in faith and knowledge through personal study.

Each lesson includes several distinctive features which we believe will benefit teachers and also serve well for personal devotional reading:

- **Biblical texts included:** Including the most relevant biblical passages within the body of each chapter allows for convenient reference to the verses under discussion. The *Doctrina* series is based primarily on the English Standard Version (ESV).

- **Footnotes for quick and convenient reference:** We believe the presence of footnotes can significantly enhance the teacher's and the reader's experience by allowing the quick identification of references to other helpful resources. We intend footnotes in this series to serve predominantly for reference and, when necessary, brief explanation.

- **Thought to Remember:** Each lesson begins with a main idea, that serves to introduce the general topic of the lesson.

- **"A Closer Look" sections:** These sections, present in many lessons, include technical material which relate, for example, to biblical languages, relevant ancient near-eastern or Greco-Roman customs, and the like. These sections are intended to shed further light on a given topic which enables teachers and readers to go deeper with a particular subject.

- **In-chapter discussion questions:** Thoughtful, open-ended questions tend to generate substantive interaction between the teacher and class members as well as meaningful reflection on the material at hand for the individual reader. In other studies, discussion questions are often placed at the end of each chapter, almost as an afterthought, making it difficult to integrate them into the lesson itself. To maximize their benefit, we have chosen to integrate open-ended discussion questions throughout each lesson in order to facilitate class discussion and personal reflection.

- **Key Ideas:** At the end of each lesson, these points help to summarize key ideas from the lesson for readers and students to remember.

- **"Discipleship Prompt" sections:** To encourage personal application and spiritual formation, we include a "Discipleship Prompt," often though not always at the end of each chapter. These prompts are intended to give the teacher and reader specific suggestions for implementing meaningful spiritual practices.

- **Prayer:** Each lesson closes with a prayer, asking God to help us incorporate the teachings of the lesson into our lives in a meaningful way.

PREFACE

I am grateful to Keith Stanglin, the Executive Director of the Center for Christian Studies, for the invitation to write this book. As a student, he was my Graduate Assistant at Harding University Graduate School of Religion (now Harding School of Theology). He has excelled his teacher in his scholarly work.

The year 2023 is the year of my retirement. I began teaching full-time in schools of theology and universities associated with churches of Christ in 1982 at Alabama Christian School of Religion (now Amridge University, 1982-1989) in Montgomery, Alabama. I then spent two years at Magnolia Bible College (1989-1991) in Kosciusko, Mississippi, followed by nine years at Harding University Graduate School of Religion (1991-2000) in Memphis, Tennessee. I have now completed my last year of full-time employment at Lipscomb University (2000-2023) in Nashville, Tennessee. God has truly blessed me in each of these institutions. Many students, colleagues, and administrators from every institution are my friends. I honor their ministries and work. I thank God for these forty years.

While writing this book, I remembered conversations, classroom lectures and questions, Bible classes and seminars at various churches, and appreciative as well as critical reviews of past books from congregants, ministers, and academics. My interest in this topic spans my whole teaching career. I began to teach academic classes on baptism and the Lord's Supper in the 1980s. So many have helped me. I owe so much to so many friends, especially students. This material will sound familiar to them (if they remember the classes or read my previous books!). I credit them with probing and honing my thoughts. Yet, of course, all errors are my own.

I offer this Bible class study book as a gift to the church that has nurtured me throughout the years. I regard it as a fruit of my academic labors. Those labors were always, to my mind, in service to God and the church.

May 13, 2023
John Mark Hicks

INTRODUCTION

Given the title of this book, I imagine two questions jump out. First, why are these *three* practices grouped together? Second, why do I call them "transforming encounters"?

At the beginning of the American Restoration Movement (also called the Stone-Campbell Movement), with which churches of Christ are associated, there was a strong emphasis on the restoration of the "ancient order" of Christianity found in the New Testament. Thomas Campbell and his son Alexander Campbell both believed baptism, the Lord's day (assembly), and the Lord's Supper were the most important public Christian institutions. Thomas, for example, wrote: "Here, then, are the three grand comprehensive positive ordinances of the gospel: namely, Baptism, the Lord's Supper, and the Lord's Day." These gospel "ordinances," he explained, were "designed to keep the blissful subject of our present and eternal salvation, in its causes, effects, and consequences, before our minds: and one day every week publicly set apart for those joyful purposes."[1]

Alexander also called them the "positive ordinances of the Christian system." He believed they were "indispensable provisions of remedial mercy" and "not one of them can be dispensed with by any who desire the perfection of the Christian state and of the Christian character."[2] Each is rooted in the "death, burial and resurrection of

---

[1] Thomas Campbell, "An Address to All our Christian Brethren, Upon the Necessity and Importance of the Actual Enjoyment of our Holy Religion," *Millennial Harbinger,* Third Series 1, no. 5 (May 1844) 202.

[2] Alexander Campbell, *Christian Baptism with its Antecedents and Consequents* (Bethany: Campbell, 1851) 246-47.

13

Christ," the "grounds of justification and hope."[3] They are both gospel and "catholic" (universal) ordinances.[4] In other words, They are "*means of grace*" through which "the hand of God" writes upon our hearts the character of the Son.[5]

This emphasis on baptism, the Lord's day (Assembly), and the Lord's Supper is part of the DNA of the Restoration Movement. Speaking at the centennial celebration of Thomas Campbell's *Declaration and Address* in 1909, Carey Morgan reflected this embedded perspective. "There are three such memorials: the Lord's Supper, Baptism and the Lord's Day. The Lord's Supper is a memorial of his death, Baptism is a symbol of his burial, and the Lord's Day celebrates his resurrection."[6]

Consequently, I have grouped these three "ordinances" together because it is part of my own heritage among churches of Christ and the Restoration Movement. But the grouping is not mere nostalgia. There is a gospel connection between these three practices. I hope the rest of the book will make that clear.

One of those connections is this: they are transformative encounters. This raises the second question: what are "transforming encounters"?

These practices are "means of grace." In other words, they are appointed means by which God graces believers. God does something through these "ordinances." But what does God do?

God encounters us. This is rather vague language, to be sure. Nevertheless, it suggests God meets us in a special way through these practices. Through them, God is present in a way God is not present in other ways. For example, when I swim in the ocean and enjoy the

---

[3] Robert Richardson, *Memoirs of Alexander Campbell* (Philadelphia: J. B. Lippincott & Co., 1870) 2:223-24.

[4] Alexander Campbell, "Dialogue on Heresy," *Millennial Harbinger* 3 (August 1832) 404.

[5] Alexander Campbell, "Regeneration," *Millennial Harbinger Extra* 4 (August 1833) 341.

[6] Carey Morgan, "The Place of the Lord's Supper in the Movement," *Centennial Convention Report*, ed. W. R. Warren (Cincinnati: Standard, 1910) 464.

goodness of God's creation, I may even experience God in that moment. Creation mediates the presence of God such that we can know God, in some sense, through the creation. At the same time, baptism in water cannot be reduced to that; it is more than that. Baptism is a *gospel* "ordinance" that unites us with the death and resurrection of Jesus. It is the experience of new creation. We experience God through baptism because of new creation, even as baptism also affirms the present goodness of creation by using water.

Something similar is true for the Lord's Supper. While we celebrate many meals together as friends and families and enjoy the goodness of God's creation through food and drink, the Lord's Supper is a *gospel* "ordinance" that participates in the body and blood of the Lord through bread and the fruit of the vine. Once again, it affirms the goodness of creation by using bread and the fruit of the vine, but it also celebrates the arrival of new creation through the body and blood of the Lord. Further, while we gather with friends, families, or communities to celebrate birthdays, anniversaries, or national holidays and enjoy God's gift of community, the assembly (or "Lord's Day") is a *gospel* "ordinance" that ushers us into the throne room of God. There, as a community, we stand in the presence of God with the angels, martyrs and other witnesses, and the whole church around the world assembled before God. As embodied persons, we gather as embodied persons in this good creation to participate in the new creation assembly gathered around God's throne.

Moreover, these encounters are transformative. This is their ultimate purpose. When God encounters us through these practices, we respond with praise, thanksgiving, and joy. At the same time, since this is a divine encounter, God is also doing something. God is not passive as if a mere spectator. On the contrary, God is working to effect the redemptive goal: to conform us to the image of Christ (Rom 8:29-30).

As flawed human beings, we confess our sinfulness. We are not all that we should be. As Romans 3:23 says, "all have sinned and fall short of the glory of God." Though we were created in the image of God (Gen 1:26-27) and crowned with glory and honor (Psa 8:5), we have all missed the mark. We have all failed to image God in our lives. In other words, we all need transformation. The work of God in Christ by the Spirit is to transform us into the glorious image of Christ (2 Cor 3:18).

These practices—baptism, assembly, and the Lord's Supper—are designed to further our transformation into that image. They are designed to renew and form our minds, hearts, and actions so that we become more like Christ. But how does that work? Is this too high a calling for these practices? I don't think so, but we'll see.

I am thankful you have chosen to read, study, and discuss these practices. May God bless this journey through the story of God in Israel, Jesus, and the church as we seek to understand these "transforming encounters."

The following resources will enhance this study and provide more detailed discussions, if desired:

- John Mark Hicks, *Come to the Table: Revisioning the Lord's Supper* (Orange, CA: New Leaf Books, 2002).

- John Mark Hicks and Greg Taylor, *Down in the River to Pray: Revisioning Baptism as God's Transforming Work* (Siloam Springs, AR: Leafwood Publishers, 2004).

- John Mark Hicks, Johnny Melton, and Bobby Valentine, *A Gathered People: Revisioning the Assembly as Transforming Encounter* (Abilene, TX: Leafwood Publishers, 2007).

- John Mark Hicks, *Enter the Water, Come to the Table: Baptism and the Lord's Supper in the Bible's Story of New Creation* (Abilene, TX: Leafwood Publishers, 2014).

− 1 −

WHAT DO WE CALL THESE COMMANDMENTS?

Matthew 3:13-17; 16:16-18; 18:15-20; 26:26-29; 28:18-20

Baptism, assembly, and the Lord's Supper are personal and communal moments through which God encounters and transforms us as we participate in the story of God.

Unfortunately, "commandment" has become an ugly word. To be sure, it has been used in abusive ways to manipulate people or to support a legalistic understanding of the Christian Faith. Nevertheless, it is still a good word. As disciples of Jesus, we are committed followers of Jesus who himself obeyed the Father (Heb 5:8; Phil 2:8). Consequently, we are called to obey. "If you love me," Jesus said, "you will keep my commandments" (John 14:15).

Since Jesus is Lord, we ought to stress obedience. At the same time, it is also important to stress the nature of that obedience. It is neither mere compliance with rules nor meaningless duties to perform. Rather, divine commands invite us to participate in the story of God. More specifically, Jesus calls us to follow him into his ministry so that we might participate in his mission. The commands, then, become moments of discipleship. They express the meaning of discipleship. These commands embody what God values and how God wants to form people into the image of Christ. They are means by which we participate in the story of God, particularly the ministry of Jesus.

This book focuses on the commands to baptize in water, assemble as a people, and eat and drink together at the table of the Lord. This chapter uses the Gospel of Matthew to identify these commands. It then raises the question of how we might name them. Is there a term that groups these three commands together in a helpful way?

The Commandments in the Gospel of Matthew

The Gospel of Matthew was probably written for a Jewish community who confessed Jesus as the Messiah. Its five teaching blocks function as a catechesis for believers similar to the five books of Moses, the Torah (chapters 5-7, 10, 13, 18, and 23-24). Matthew's Gospel disciples this community in terms of ethics, theology, and practices.

In Matthew, Jesus gathers an assembly (church) that prays together, eats together, and makes disciples by baptizing and teaching the nations to observe everything Jesus commanded. All three practices studied in this book—baptism, assembly, and the Lord's Supper—are present in Matthew's Gospel. In fact, only this Gospel uses the term "church" (*ekklesia*; 16:18; 18:17). The Gospel of Matthew intends, in part, to form believers into a healthy assembly of God's baptized people who sit at table together as they participate in the mission and ministry of Jesus.

> As you read each section, ask how baptism, assembly, and the Lord's Supper are rooted in the ministry and teaching of Jesus in the Gospel of Matthew.

MATTHEW 3:15; 28:19

15 *Jesus answered him, "Let it be so now, for thus it is fitting for us to fulfill all righteousness."*

19 *"Go therefore and make disciples of all nations, baptizing them in the name of the Father and of the Son and of the Holy Spirit."*

Baptism

At the beginning of the Gospel of Matthew, John baptized Jesus (3:13-17). At its end, Jesus commissioned his disciples to make disciples of all nations, baptizing them and teaching them (28:18-20).

Jesus understood baptism as a command. His baptism, Jesus said, would "fulfill all righteousness" (3:15). Jesus did what was required and did it in solidarity with the people of Israel who came to be baptized by John (3:6). The resurrected Lord extended the practice of baptism in making disciples. If Jesus was baptized, his followers will be baptized as well. If we are disciples of Jesus, then we will follow Jesus into the water.

In the Great Commission, Jesus commands his followers to continue his discipling ministry through (1) baptism and (2) teaching. As Christ-followers, we practice and teach what Jesus practiced and taught in his own life and ministry. Discipling the nations has created communities of Jesus-followers scattered around the world. These communities, then, not only baptize but also teach new disciples to "observe all that" Jesus had "commanded" them. That includes baptism as well as assembling and sharing in the Lord's table.

The specific command in Matthew 28:19a is to "make disciples of all nations." As the followers of Jesus scattered across the world from Jerusalem, they discipled people among the nations, "baptizing them in the name of the Father and of the Son, and of the Holy Spirit, teaching them to observe all that I have commanded you" (28:19b-20a). Whether the Greek participles are instrumental ("make disciples by baptizing") or circumstantial ("make disciples in the context of baptizing"), the result is the same: the formation of a baptized community (or church) of Jesus-followers who obey the commandments of Jesus.

We are baptized into (Greek: *eis*) the communion or name of the Father, Son, and Spirit. This is a movement into the community of the Father, Son, and Spirit. To be baptized "into the name" signifies belonging to and identifying with the one named. Through baptism, we enter a relationship with the divine community (Trinity, or Triune God) where we belong to God's communion, share God's mission, and honor the "name" (identity) of God. In baptism, we are identified by our communion with the name, that is, our communion is with the Father, Son, and Spirit. We belong!

A CLOSER LOOK: "BAPTIZED INTO..."

The Greek word *eis* can often be translated "into," having a spatial meaning. In Gal 3:27, Paul says "For as many of you as were baptized into Christ have put on Christ" (ESV). In this verse, Paul indicates that we have been brought into union with Christ through baptism. This is also the most likely meaning of Paul's statement in Rom 6:3, "Do you not know that all of us who have been baptized into Christ Jesus were baptized into his death?" (ESV).[7]

MATTHEW 16:16; 18:19-20

16 *And I tell you, you are Peter, and on this rock I will build my church, and the gates of hell shall not prevail against it.*

19 *Again I say to you, if two of you agree on earth about anything they ask, it will be done for them by my Father in heaven.* 20 *For where two or three are gathered in my name, there am I among them.*

Assembly

This community of baptized Jesus-followers, united in their communion with the Triune God, is called "church." This English word translates the Greek word *ekklēsia*, which primarily means "assembly." Assembly is its typical meaning in Greco-Roman culture and in the New Testament (Acts 19:32, 39; 1 Cor 14:23).

When Peter confessed Jesus as the Messiah in Matthew 16:16, Jesus immediately followed with the declaration that "on this rock I

---

[7] For more on this, see Douglas Moo, *The Epistle to the Romans*, NICNT (Grand Rapids: Eerdmans, 1996), 360.

will build my church" (*ekklēsia*; 16:18). In other words, Jesus will build his church (assembly) on the foundation (or rock) of his messianic identity.

Because *ekklēsia* is translated as "church," it is easy to miss its fuller significance. Israel is called an "assembly of the LORD" (*ekklēsia kyriou*) in the Greek translation of the Hebrew Scriptures (Deut 23:2-4, 9; Judg 21:5). Israel also gathered to worship God in assemblies (2 Chr 5:12-13; Psa 22:22, 25). Stephen identified Israel as the *ekklēsia* (church) in the wilderness (Acts 7:38).

Jesus is making a bold claim. He will renew the assembly of Israel under his Lordship. It is the church of Jesus ("my church"), or the church of the Messiah. The assembly of Israel will belong to Israel's Messiah. Jesus will renew the assembly of Israel as the church of the Messiah (Christ).

The community of Jesus-followers, then, will become an assembly of the Messiah, and this assembly will gather as a people. There is no church if people never assemble. The church is a gathered people who live out their faith in community and as a community. This is what Jesus himself did. Jesus attended weekly assemblies as he went to the synagogue every sabbath (Luke 4:16). He also participated in the communal festivals of Israel (Passover, Feast of Tabernacles, Feast of Lights, etc.). Jesus, in effect, went to church (assembly) and lived out his faith in community.

Jesus expects his church (*ekklēsia*) to do the same. They gather as a church (Matt 18:17). While the context of Matthew 18:15-20 is specific, the principle in verses 19-20 is broad. The process of reconciliation within a community is a specific application of a larger principle. The principle applies beyond that setting.

The principle is this: whenever disciples "are gathered in (*eis*; into) my name, there am I among them" (Matt 18:20). Disciples gather into the name of Jesus, that is, they gather as people belonging to Jesus. They are the assembly of the Messiah. When believers devoted to following Jesus gather (assemble) to pray (worship), Jesus is present among them. He is Immanuel in their midst even when he is no longer present in the flesh.

Gathering into the name of Jesus is assembling in the presence of Jesus who assures us of God's good news for us. The presence of Jesus is the divine assurance of God's faithful commitment. God listens to the gathered community because Jesus is present.

MATTHEW 26:26b, 27b-28

26b *"Take, eat: this is my body."*

27b *"Drink of it, all of you,* 28 *for this is my blood of the covenant, which is poured out for many for the forgiveness of sins."*

The Lord's Supper

Jesus institutes the Lord's Supper at his last Passover with his disciples (Matt 26:17-19). The Passover tells the story of Israel's liberation from Egypt and invites participants to experience anew that liberation. They remember their first Passover and celebrate their deliverance from Egyptian enslavement.

In this meal, Jesus gave the Passover a fuller meaning (cf. Luke 22:16). This fuller meaning includes our participation in the body and blood of Jesus as we eat and drink with the living Jesus in the kingdom of God (1 Cor 10:16-17). Jesus intended for his disciples to continue the practice of eating and drinking in the kingdom with Jesus (Matt 26:29; "I will drink it new with you in my Father's kingdom"). It celebrates the new covenant where the forgiveness of sins and communion with God are experienced anew at the table.

This expectation is more explicit in Luke's account. Specifically, Jesus says, "Do this in remembrance of me" (Luke 22:19). The imperative, "do this," is a command. Participation in the Lord's Table, eating and drinking with Jesus, is a command. The assembly of Israel's Messiah is expected to gather as a community—whether as a whole or in smaller groups—to eat and drink together in remembrance of what God has done in Jesus.

Ordinances, Sacraments, or Both?

The Gospel of Matthew embeds these three practices within the ministry of Jesus. Consequently, followers of Jesus are baptized, they assemble and sit at table together, just like Jesus.

The Restoration Movement called these practices "positive ordinances." Several traditions within Christian history, especially Baptists and Mennonites, have called these commandments "ordinances." Derived from Latin, the term suggests a legal order or arrangement. One of the agendas of the Restoration Movement was to restore the "ancient order," that is, the ancient ordinances according to the commandments of the Lord.

Most other traditions have used the word "sacrament" to describe these commandments. This term also has a Latin origin (*sacramentum*). It means an oath or a mystery. Tertullian (ca. AD 200) is the first known Christian writer to use it (*On the Crown*, 9, 13). He used it in the sense of an oath of allegiance. The Roman Catholic tradition as well as some Protestant traditions (Lutherans and Anglicans, for example) use the word "sacrament" to categorize these commandments in the sense of "mystery" more than "oath" (though the number of "sacraments" varies). In fact, Eastern Orthodoxy, especially the Greek Orthodox Church, identifies them as "the Holy Mysteries," using the Greek term *mysteria*.

While we could simply call them commandments, perhaps it is helpful to tease out their meaning with healthy identifiers. Ordinance is helpful because these practices are commanded so that the church might become what God intended it to be. We are invited to participate in God's story by obeying these commands. We are baptized, we assemble, and we eat at the Lord's Table.

But is the word "sacrament" helpful? The Restoration Movement typically rejected the term. The word carries negative baggage for many. Some associate it with magical powers or something similar. Others associate it with works-righteousness. Still others think it suggests the effect of the practice is automatic as if God does not care about faith but only the act itself. Though these objections are often misunderstandings, they do impede a healthy understanding of the term.

Why do many prefer the term "ordinance" instead of "sacrament," or vice versa? What are the benefits, dangers, or irrelevancy of such a discussion?

However, is there anything valuable in its use? To put it simply, *while "ordinance" emphasizes what the believers do, "sacrament" emphasizes what God does.* Of course, it is both/and, and while neither term is necessary, they are both helpful. One stresses our obedience, and the other stresses God's faithful work.

If we use the word sacrament, what is gained? It stresses the mysterious work of God through baptism, assembly, and the Lord's Supper. Through these practices, God encounters us for the sake of our transformation into the image of God. What God does in them is, by the power of the Spirit, transformative. Using the word "sacrament" reminds us that God is at work through these practices. They are not merely ordinances of human obedience but also divine acts of mercy and transformation!

If we affirm this both/and (we do something in these practices and God also does something), it might be helpful to fill in this picture a bit more fully. What are we really saying about them? In essence, this is my fundamental point: *because of the work of Christ and by the power of the Spirit, God graces and blesses us through material symbols of water, gathering, and bread and the fruit of the vine, when by faith we participate in the past, present, and future story of God through baptism, assembly, and Lord's Supper.*[8]

---

[8] For a fuller discussion of the definition of a sacrament, see John Mark Hicks, Johnny Melton, and Bobby Valentine, *A Gathered People: Revisioning the Assembly as Transforming Encounter* (Abilene, TX: Leafwood Publishers, 2007), 12, 141-143; John Mark Hicks, *Enter the Water, Come to the Table: Baptism and the Lord's Supper in Scripture's Story of New Creation* (Abilene: Abilene University Press, 2014), 12-14. On "eschatological," see *Enter the Water, Come to Table*, pp. 99-118.

That needs some unpacking. The following bullet points expand the brief definition:

- **Material Creation:** these commandments are embodied practices with concrete connections to God's good creation. We are baptized in water; people gather as living, breathing creatures; and we eat bread and drink the fruit of the vine at the table. God graces these good gifts (water, bread, the fruit of the vine, and bodies) and gives them new meaning in the community of Christ-followers.

- **Symbol:** these practices not only point to their meaning but also participate in their meaning. These symbols point beyond themselves to the reality of God's salvation and participate in the reality itself.

- **Means of Grace:** these symbols are instruments of God's grace. God graces and blesses the people of God through these practices. They are appointed means and connected to explicit divine promises.

- **Eschatological** (pertaining to God's goal in the present and in the future): we experience the future through these practices. Baptism is no mere bath; it is a participation in the death and resurrection of Jesus as well as a promise of our own future resurrection. Assembly is no mere social gathering; it is an encounter with the God who sits on the heavenly throne with all the saints in glory. The Lord's Supper is no mere meal; it is eating with the living Christ who hosts the Messianic banquet.

- **Through Faith:** we receive God's work through trusting in what God has done in Christ. We do not earn God's grace in these practices; we receive what God gives.

- **By the Power of the Spirit:** God acts through the Spirit to work God's gracious intent. The practices do not, in and of themselves, have any power but are only efficacious by the Spirit's work.

- **Christ-Centered:** these practices are grounded in the work of God in Christ rather than in any work we do. They are directed by Christ, rooted in Christ, and serve the purpose to form us into the image of Christ.

What is helpful or problematic about the definition of "sacrament" offered? Do you have any misgivings with the definition?

There are, then, at least two dimensions to these practices. First, they are ordinances. God has commanded the use of these practices for our own good, both individually and communally. They are part of the "order" that God envisions for the church. We obey these commandments. As ordinances, it is legitimate to ask, *what are we to do and why?*

Second, *they are sacraments or mysteries* (you may use a different word if you desire). They are means by which God, in part, effects our transformation through our participation in the gospel as a community. Through baptism, assembly, and the Lord's Supper, God encounters us. God meets us in these practices for our sake. God does something in us, for us, and among us through them. As sacraments, it is legitimate to ask, *what is God doing?*

How does the affirmation of both ordinance and sacrament deepen your thinking about baptism, assembly, and the Lord's Supper?

Throughout this book, we will ask both questions about these three commandments. What is God doing, and how do we participate?

KEY IDEAS:

• Though some tend to relegate these practices to addendums to the Christian Faith, they are embedded in the story of Jesus who expects his disciples to follow his directives.

- While we often think about these divine commandments as primarily something we do, they are more fundamentally something God does.

- The language of "sacrament" can reorient our thinking away from individualistic human-centered obedience to communal God-centered participation in the story of God.

DISCIPLESHIP PROMPT:

Disciples follow Jesus. They keep his commandments, and those commands are rooted in the ministry of Jesus. Jesus paved the way. He was baptized, and we follow him into the water. He assembled with the people of God, and we follow him into the assemblies of God's people. He sat at table with his disciples, and we follow him by sitting at table with his disciples. We follow Jesus by obeying his commands, and Jesus promises to grace his disciples with forgiveness, presence, and strength through these practices. As we begin this study, reflect on your own life: have you followed Jesus into the water? Do you follow Jesus by regularly assembling with God's people? Do you follow Jesus by sharing the Lord's Supper with fellow disciples?

PRAYER:

God, give us the mind to understand your commands, the heart to submit to them, and the strength to do them. We praise you for these gifts. By them you enlighten our understanding, humble our hearts, and empower us with your grace. In the name of Jesus, Amen.

– 2 –

ISRAEL—BAPTIZED INTO MOSES IN THE CLOUD AND IN THE SEA

1 Corinthians 10:1-2; Leviticus 15; Hebrews 10:22

> **Israel has its own baptismal journey by which God redeems and cleanses a people for God's own possession and mission.**

In the beginning, the Spirit of God hovered over dark chaotic waters (Gen 1:1-2). In love, God brought order to that chaos. God created a good earth and filled it with good gifts. Out of the waters (chaos), God fashioned a habitation where humanity could multiply and flourish. As images of God, human beings were invited to participate in the divine mission to fill the earth with God's glory, subdue the remaining chaos, and shepherd the earth (Gen 1:28).

However, humanity substituted its own mission for God's mission. They created an alternative story rather than embracing God's goal. Exiled from the garden and living east of Eden, humanity quickly degenerated from fratricide (Gen 4:9) to global violence (Gen 6:11-13). Ultimately, humanity adopted an idolatrous agenda where they intended to make a name for themselves rather than honoring God's name. They responded to God's word, "Let us make" humanity "in our image," in Gen 1:26 with their own agenda, "let us make a name for ourselves" in Gen 11:4.[9]

---

[9] For a fuller explanation of this paragraph, see John Mark Hicks, *Around the Bible in 80 Days: The Story of God from Creation to New Creation* (Abilene: Leafwood Publishers, 2022), 25-56.

In response, God graciously elected Abraham and promised to "bless" him. God decided to make his "name great" so that "all the families of the earth" might be blessed (Gen 12:2-3). Amid the chaos humanity produced upon the earth, God decided to create a new people who would represent God in the world and participate in God's mission as a light to the nations. However, before that great nation became a reality, the descendants of Abraham were enslaved in Egypt where they suffered oppression for hundreds of years. God heard their groanings for help, and ultimately God "remembered his covenant with Abraham" (Exod 2:23-24). God decided to redeem Israel.

---

1 CORINTHIANS 10:1-2

1 For I do not want you to be unaware, brothers, that our fathers were all under the cloud, and all passed through the sea, 2 and all were baptized into Moses in the cloud and in the sea.

Baptized in the Cloud and in the Sea

God redeemed Israel through the sea and the cloud. Paul names the cloud and sea twice in the space of two verses. This underscores their importance. Israel "passed through the sea" and "under the cloud." In other words, they were baptized "in the cloud and in the sea."

The cloud is the presence of God. The Lord led Israel "in a pillar of cloud" which became "a pillar of fire" at night (Exod 13:21; Neh 9:11; Psa 105:39). This pillar surrounded Israel as it "moved from before them and stood behind them" (Exod 14:19). Moreover, the glory of the Lord appears "in the cloud" (Exod 16:10). When Israel saw the cloud, they knew God was with them, leading them, and protecting them (Exod 14:24). The cloud testified to God's faithful presence.

The sea, however, was a threat. It blocked Israel's escape from the Egyptian army. Also, the sea was a form of the chaotic waters that threatened dry land and terrified sailors. The "waters" that covered the earth in darkness in Gen 1:2 obstructed Israel's path to freedom (Exod 14:21-22; 15:8; Psa 78:13-14). When Israel had their backs to the sea, they needed deliverance. But the sea was no obstacle to God but a path to liberation. Israel walked to freedom on dry land "through the sea" (Exod 14:16, 29), "through the great waters" (Psa 77:19). God delivered them from slavery and death through the chaos of the waters. At the same time, those same "waters" destroyed Israel's enemy (Exod 15:10, 19).

Paul describes this moment as a baptism "into Moses in the cloud and in the sea." Surrounded by the cloud on all sides—back, front, and above, they passed through the sea surrounded by water on both sides (Exod 14:29). In other words, they were immersed (baptized) in the cloud and in the sea. God was present in the cloud and protected Israel from the waters as well as the Egyptian army. Israel passed from death to life as God's presence enveloped them. They moved from slavery to freedom because God liberated them through the sea. God redeemed Israel through the waters (Exod 6:6; 15:13; 1 Chr 17:21).

By this means, God created a people with a new identity ("into Moses"). Some suggest the Hebrew verb *qanah* ("purchased" in Exod 15:16) alludes to giving birth (see Deut 32:6; Psa 74:2; 139:13). Cain's name is derived from this verb, and Eve named him Cain because she had "gotten a man with the help of the LORD" (Gen 4:1). Out of the chaos of the waters, God gave birth to Israel, who became God's "firstborn son" (Exod 4:22). One might say, like the language of John 3:5, Israel was born again in water (sea) and the Spirit (cloud). Moreover, the Song of Moses uses the language of the kinsmen redeemer: "the people whom you have redeemed" (Exod 15:13). With steadfast love, God rescued a kinsman, a people (Exod 6:6).

Why does Paul call this a baptism? He uses the same phrase "baptized into" in reference to Moses that he uses in reference to Jesus (Rom 6:3; Gal 3:27). The point of the comparison may be something like this: just as we are baptized into union with Christ and under the leadership of Christ, so Israel was baptized into the community Moses led. Just as we are identified with Jesus in our crossing from death to life, so Israel was identified with Moses in their crossing of the sea. Israel, led by Moses, was baptized in the cloud and in water, and we, led by Christ, are baptized in the Holy Spirit and in water (1 Cor 6:11;

12:13; Titus 3:5). God gave Israel a new identity in their baptism, and Christ gives us a new identity in ours.

How do we experience the Exodus in our own baptism? What does the song of Exodus 15 mean for us and our celebration of baptism?

This language immerses Christians in Israel's history. The church is a continuation of the story of Israel. Just as Israel was baptized into Moses, so the church is baptized into Israel's Messiah. The story of God's redemptive work in Israel continues among the nations through Gentile Christians. They are part of that story. The God of Abraham, Isaac, and Jacob is also the God of the Gentiles. They are "our fathers," too.

HEBREWS 10:22

[22] *Let us draw near with a true heart in full assurance of faith, with our hearts sprinkled clean from an evil conscience and our bodies washed with pure water.*

Baptisms in Israel

Hebrews 10, which we will consider in some detail in chapter twelve, draws an analogy between the ritual of the High Priest on Israel's Day of Atonement (Yom Kippur) and our Christian experience of salvation. On that day, the High Priest entered the Holy of Holies twice to sprinkle blood on the ark of the covenant, once for himself and the second time for the people. As Israel fasted and prayed, the High Priest represented Israel in the Holy of Holies. There God heard Israel's penitent cries for forgiveness.

Before the High Priest entered the Holy of Holies, he prepared himself by putting on the proper clothes, a sash around his waist, and a special turban on his head. Prior to clothing himself, however, he "bathe[d] his body in water" (Lev 16:4). This ritual immersion in water cleansed the body before entering the presence of the Holy One. The High Priest presented himself as clean before God.

Hebrews 10:22 alludes to this moment. Like the High Priest, we draw near to God with authentic faith having been cleansed by blood and water. Just as the High Priest sprinkled the blood of animals on the ark, so our hearts have been sprinkled with the blood of Jesus. Just as the High Priest washed his body in water, so our bodies have been "washed with pure water." As believers in the Messiah, we enter the Holy of Holies through the death of Christ. Our High Priest grants access to the Most Holy Place as we draw near in faith with hearts sprinkled by the atoning blood of Jesus and with bodies washed in pure water. Hebrews 10:22 uses the same language as Lev 16:4: bodies are washed (bathed) in water.

Reflecting on Heb 10:22, what elements are important for your understanding of your own baptism?

This practice immersed the "whole body in water" (Lev 15:16). The covenant required a cleansing ritual for many different situations. Leviticus 15 identifies some of these occasions (also Lev 14:8-9), including touching a dead body or anything unclean. The Torah prescribes immersion in water as the means for cleansing the body from physical defilement and reaffirming one's commitment to the holiness of God. This cleansing enabled people to come to the place of God's dwelling and once again join the community in worship. This embodied practice provided a way of pursuing sanctification for both body and spirit. One danger, however, is the substitution of the cleansing of the body for the cleansing of the soul. Nevertheless, water rituals were part of what it meant to live a holy life in Israel.

During the time of Jesus, devout Jews continued these immersion rituals. They practiced them in ancient Jewish baptistries called *mikva'ot* (singular: *mikveh*). They were located near synagogues, in home basements, and hundreds surrounded the temple itself. Priests, for example, immersed themselves before entering the temple. Luke

11:38 may allude to the frequent practice of this ritual. A Pharisee was surprised when Jesus did not first wash himself before eating. The verb "washed" is from the Greek word *baptō*, which typically means to immerse. In other words, the Pharisee was surprised that Jesus did not first immerse (bathe himself in water) before sitting down at the table to eat (though some suggest it only refers to dipping one's hands in water). Mark 7:4 also suggests how pervasive these rituals were in Jewish life. Devoted followers of the traditions even immersed or baptized (*baptizō*) their cups, pots, and other vessels.

The term *baptismos* (baptism) sometimes identifies these water ablutions. For example, the preacher in Hebrews uses the term twice. One of the fundamentals of the faith is proper instruction about "washings" (baptisms) along with the laying of hands, faith and repentance, and the resurrection of the dead and eternal judgment (Heb 6:1-2). In other words, if one is to progress in the Christian faith, one must have some sense of the difference between Jewish ritual baptisms and Christian baptism. The Mosaic covenant, according to Heb 9:10, was filled with "various washings" (*baptismos*). They served a cleansing purpose and purified people for entrance into the holy presence of God in daily life and at the temple.

These water rituals were no *mere* ceremonies; they provided communal and social boundaries for holiness. They served a meaningful purpose as part of shared communal life and devotion to God. These water cleansings lead us to the baptism of John who immersed Jesus (as we will see in chapter five). Ultimately, they introduce us to Christian baptism where the baptismal journey in Israel finds its ultimate fulfillment. Israel's water cleansings are types of Christian baptism. As noted above, like Israel's High Priest, we too enter the Most Holy Place after our bodies have been washed in pure water (Heb 10:22) and our hearts sprinkled with blood. As priests, we enter the Holy of Holies with cleansed bodies and souls as we are washed in pure water and our hearts are sprinkled with the blood of Jesus.

How do Israel's water immersions enhance your own understanding of Christianity's baptism?

Throughout church history, from the beginning until only the recent past, baptism was required for full participation in the assemblies of God's people, particularly communion at the Lord's table. Church architecture reflects the importance of this practice. While many later buildings installed a baptismal font before the altar or at an entrance to the building, some sanctuaries were constructed without baptistries because the baptistry was a separate building altogether. Two famous examples in Italy are the Duomos (Cathedrals) in Pisa and Florence. This symbolizes the priority of baptism before gathering at the table. Historically, only the baptized fully participate in the holy table of the Lord. Further, most liturgical churches (for example, Roman Catholics and Anglicans) have a font filled with water inside the entrance of the sanctuary. There people can dip their hands, sprinkle themselves, reminding themselves of their baptism as they gather with the community in the presence of God.

These structures and practices remind us that we enter the presence of God through our cleansing—our hearts sprinkled with the blood of Christ and our bodies washed in pure water.

Israel's Baptism and Ours

How might Israel's baptism into Moses and their subsequent baptismal practices shape our own practice of baptism? This is a legitimate question because there is continuity in God's grand narrative. Baptism is something Israel shares with Christian believers.

Our baptism, like Israel's, is embedded in a story of redemption. God remembered the covenant with Abraham, heard the cry of the people, and acted to redeem them. Their Exodus from Egypt is part of a larger story. When they crossed the sea, they assumed an identity as a people baptized into Moses. When they celebrate the Exodus, they retell that story and reimagine themselves as participants in that moment.

35

Baptism into Christ unites us with the story of Israel through its Messiah. We become part of that bigger story. It is important to rehearse that story for the candidate of baptism as well as for the community who witnesses it. Our baptism testifies to the story of God in Christ who redeems in the power of the Spirit. Baptism reminds us that we are now identified with Israel. Their story is our story. Abraham is now our ancestor through the Messiah. We share a common identity as the people of God; we have been grafted into Israel's tree (Rom 11:17).

Our baptism, like Israel's, is an occasion for great celebration. When Israel reached the other side of the sea and God released the chaotic waters on their enemy, Israel celebrated. They sang the Song of Moses, and Miriam led the nation in celebration with music and song (Exod 15:20-21). Israel passed from death to life, from enslavement to liberation. They rejoiced and celebrated God's steadfast love and faithfulness.

Baptism into Christ is an occasion for great celebration. We, too, have passed from death to life, from enslavement to liberation. Let us surround this moment with song, prayer, thanksgiving, and joy. It is a birthday party! It is a communal event, though there are appropriate situations for private baptisms. As a communal practice, we might institute some practices that give the community the opportunity to celebrate this passing through the sea in the cloud.

Why is water such a dynamic and pervasive image in Israel's history and practice? How might contemporary Christians express that dynamic character in our practices?

Our baptism, like Israel's, testifies to our cleansing. At the sea, Israel escaped death and destruction. In its water rituals, Israel renewed life with God through cleansing, and that cleansing offered a path to enter God's presence with wholeness. In other words, the cleansing rituals became a means of reentering holy space. Cleansed bodies and renewed souls passed through the waters to commune with God.

Baptism into Christ is a mode of cleansing as well. Washed with pure water, we cross a divide from death to life, from enslavement to liberation. The ancient church symbolized this by taking off their old clothes for baptism and putting on new clothes after their baptism. Other traditions symbolize it by wearing white baptismal garments. Baptism is a transition from one sphere to another, from the kingdom of darkness to the kingdom of light. Our baptismal practices can stress this through appropriate symbols (whether garments or actions), words, prayers, and songs.

Our baptism, like Israel's, is the beginning of a journey into the life of God. The crossing of the sea was not the goal but a means. The goal, as we will see in the next chapter, was to bring Israel to God's abode at Mount Sinai and ultimately to the promised land. The sea-crossing began Israel's journey through the wilderness to God's dwelling place as they were led by the glory of God in the cloud and pillar of fire. That glory led them to their inheritance, the land God promised Abraham.

Baptism into Christ is also the beginning of a journey. We will travel through many tribulations and trials before we enter God's dwelling place in the new heaven and new earth. Our baptism (sea) launches this journey, anoints us with the Holy Spirit (cloud), identifies us with a community (the people of God), and equips us for the journey as God supplies what we need (like manna in the wilderness). Our baptism testifies to this journey. The community, as well as the candidate for baptism, remembers that this is the beginning of a struggle through the wilderness. Moreover, our baptism is a constant resource. For just as Israel always looked back to the crossing of the sea for courage and confidence (Psa 77:15-20; Hab 3), so we remember our baptism as a source of courage and confidence.

KEY IDEAS:

- Water baptism in Christianity has roots in the redemptive and cleansing practices of Israel.
- God's deliverance of Israel from Egypt through the sea and in the

cloud is analogous to the Christian's experience of redemption through baptism.

- The Mosaic covenant commanded the practice of water rituals to cleanse and dedicate the whole person to God, which typifies Christian baptism.

DISCIPLESHIP PROMPT:

Disciples of Jesus follow Israel's Messiah. We are part of the story of Israel, and that story continues through the Messiah's disciples. Israel's baptism invites us into the water to experience liberation from what enslaves us. The God of the Exodus is the God of Jesus. We are baptized into the story of Israel and its Messiah. Disciples embrace an appreciation of and gratitude for God's redemptive work in Israel. Consequently, Israel's baptismal experience informs our own.

As you read and study the story of Israel in the Old Testament, remember that this is a story that you have become a part of through baptism.

PRAYER:

God, thank you for including us in the story of Israel so that, in Christ, their history is also our story. Give us the grace to remember our baptism through our identification with Israel and their liberation from Egyptian bondage. In the name of Jesus, Amen.

– 3 –

ISRAEL—ASSEMBLED AT THE MOUNTAIN AND THROUGHOUT THEIR CALENDAR

Exodus 19:1-11; Leviticus 23

> **God calls Israel into frequent assemblies sanctified by divine presence.**

When God created the heavens and the earth, God blessed and commissioned humanity to "be fruitful and multiply" in order to fill the earth with God's glory through populating the earth with human beings who image and represent God (Gen 1:1, 26-28). When God called Abraham out of Mesopotamia and established his lineage, God blessed and commissioned Abraham's family to be "fruitful and multiply" (Gen 28:3; 35:11; 48:4). This blessing gave rise to a "company of peoples," or more literally, an *assembly* (Hebrew: *qahal*) of peoples. The divine promise envisions an assembly or gathering of peoples (plural). This is not the future of a single people, but the future of peoples around the world. It is the blessing of the nations. As God promised Abraham, "in you all the families of the earth shall be blessed" (Gen 12:3).

Embedded in the promise to Abraham, Isaac, and Jacob is the creation of an assembly that includes "all the families of the earth." This single assembly consists of many nations or peoples. Isaiah envisioned a time when the sworn enemies of Israel, Egypt and Assyria, would become the people of God (Isa 19:25). The time would finally come through Israel's Messiah. Paul prayed for Jews and Gentiles in Rome to "with one voice glorify the God and Father of our Lord Jesus Christ" (Rom 15:6). John saw an innumerable multitude gathered "from every nation, from all tribes and peoples and languages, standing before the throne and before the Lamb" praising God and the Lamb "with a loud voice" (Rev 7:9-10). This is the goal, that is, to unite all the peoples of the earth into one assembly praising God with one voice before the throne of God and the Lamb.

The beginning of that journey was the call of Abraham, the promise to his descendants, the liberation of Israel from enslavement in Egypt, and the trek through the wilderness to Mount Sinai where God dwelt. At the mountain of God (Exod 3:1; 24:13), Israel becomes a covenanted people. They became the assembly of the Lord, God's own congregation.

EXODUS 19:4-6

4 *You yourselves have seen what I did to the Egyptians, and how I bore you on eagles' wings and brought you to myself.* 5 *Now therefore, if you will indeed obey my voice and keep my covenant, you shall be my treasured possession among all peoples, for all the earth is mine;* 6 *and you shall be to me a kingdom of priests and a holy nation.'*

The Day of the Assembly

Some forty years after Israel assembled at Mount Sinai, Moses stood on the banks of the Jordan river and gathered Israel to hear the word of the Lord. In Deut 9-10 Moses rehearses what happened at Sinai and beyond. Though they were about to enter the land God had promised, it was neither their faithfulness nor righteousness that secured their entrance. While at God's holy mountain, Israel crafted an idol for itself. Later, they failed to trust God's promise at Kadesh and refused to take possession of the land. Despite this stubborn wickedness, God nevertheless faithfully fulfilled his promise to Abraham by leading Israel into the promised land.

What is important for this study is how Deut characterizes that day when Israel met God at Mount Sinai. On that day God spoke from the mountain, not in the voice of a human messenger like Moses, but in God's own voice. The Lord spoke to the assembled people of Israel from the holy mountain. Three times Deut describes this as "the day of the assembly" (9:10; 10:4; 18:16; cf. 5:22). On that day, Israel become the "assembly of the Lord" (cf. Deut 23:1-3, 8).

The description is significant. The "day of the assembly" is narrated in Exod 19–24. God liberated Israel from their enslavement to meet their God at Sinai. As the voice of God tells Israel through Moses (Exod 19:4), "You yourselves have seen what I did to the Egyptians, and how I bore you on eagles' wings and brought you to myself." God rescued Israel so that they might become a people who know God. On the day of the assembly, God gathered Israel at the mountain for the sake of *encounter*, *covenant-making*, and *communion*.

> **Identify some features of God's meeting with Israel on the "day of assembly" in Exod 19. What happened? Why is this significant?**

This divine-human encounter is described in dramatic terms in Exod 19. First, Israel consecrated themselves, washed their clothes, and abstained from sexual relations. They would meet God as people dedicated to holiness; a people prepared to meet their God. To meet God is nothing flippant; it is a grave moment. Second, a "thick cloud" with thunder and lightning enveloped the mountain. Smoke filled the air because Yahweh "had descended on it in fire." The mountain quaked, and the people trembled. Third, through the smoke, thunder, and fire, God appeared and spoke to the people. They heard God's voice, and it was more than the people could bear. From then on, they only wanted to hear the voice of Moses (Exod 20:1-19). Yet, the divine presence was for their sake as God tested Israel so that they might properly reverence God and avoid sin that would separate them from God's presence (Exod 20:20).

The assembly continued as Moses approached the "thick darkness" and detailed the meaning of the Ten Commandments for Israel's life (Exod 20:22–23:33). Moses spoke the words of the covenant. These words are called the "book of the covenant" (Exod 24:7; cf. 2 Kgs 23:2, 21; 2 Chr 34:30). As God invites Israel into a covenant relationship, the book of the covenant apprises Israel about what that entails for covenantal life and God's expectations for their holiness before the divine presence. The day of assembly is the day of commitment. It is the day Israel makes a covenantal vow.

On the day of the assembly, the representatives of Israel went up on the mountain to worship Yahweh. This included Moses and Aaron, Nadab and Abihu, and seventy elders of Israel (Exod 24:1, 9). Before they ascended the mountain, however, Moses took the book of the covenant and asked the people whether they would keep all the words of the covenant. The people vowed they would (Exod 24:3-4). On that day of assembly, Israel became the covenant people of God who bound themselves to the words of the covenant. The assembly was the day Israel pledged its allegiance to God.

On that day of assembly, Israel was constituted as a covenanted assembly of the Lord gathered in the presence of God. This gathering, represented by those who ascended the mountain, encountered God ("saw God") and they ate and drank in God's presence (Exod 24:9-11). While the next chapter will explore this moment more thoroughly in light of what they ate and drank, its importance for assembly is what concerns us here. This gathered, representative, group—an assembly of the Lord—communed with God on the holy mountain. They were not struck down but enjoyed God's presence. They ate and drank in God's presence.

How does Israel's "holy mountain" experience shape your understanding of the "mountain" experience of Christians in assembly? What parallels do you see? How should this inform and inspire our own assemblies?

Eventually, this divine presence would rest within Israel in the Tabernacle. This is, in fact, the goal of the book of Exodus. The last chapter records God's descent into the Tabernacle as God's resting place among the people of God (Exod 40:34-35). There God would "meet" Israel (Exod 25:22; 29:42; 30:6, 36). Consequently, it was called the "tent of meeting" (Exod 27:21; 28:43; 29:4ff). As a covenanted community, Israel would encounter God's presence at the Tabernacle for forgiveness, vows, thanksgivings, and communion. At the Tabernacle (and later the Temple), Israel regularly *encountered* God, *renewed their covenant* with God, and *communed* with God.

The day of the assembly provides the visionary framework for all subsequent assemblies of Israel. For example, the psalms assume a gathering as these prayers and hymns are sung in the space where Israel assembles to meet God. The psalmists (e.g., 22:25; 35:18; 40:9-10) commit to praise God in the "great congregation" (assembly; *qahal*) or the "assembly of" (*qahal*) God's people (Psa 89:5; 107:32; 149:1).

Israel assembled, and when they did, they encountered God. They offered their thanksgivings and renewed their vows. And they communed with God as they met God "face to face" (cf. "before the face of" God in Psa 22:27, 29; 24:6; 42:2; 50:3; 68:4; 86:9; 96:9; 98:6; 100:2).

LEVITICUS 23:2b

2b *These are the appointed feasts of the Lord that you shall proclaim as holy convocations; they are my appointed feasts.*

Israel Calendar: Regular and Frequent Assemblies

Since encounter, covenant renewal, and communion are important features of Israel's assemblies before God, it is no surprise that God invited Israel to frequent and habitual assemblies. They are enumerated in Lev 23 among other places in the Torah.

Leviticus calls them "holy convocations" or sacred assemblies (cf. Exod 12:16; Num 28:18, 25, 26; 29:1, 7, 12). They are called "holy" because every assembly of Israel was one gathered in the presence of God. They are called "convocations" because these are communal moments in the life of Israel. They do not describe individual piety but communal worship.

Leviticus 23 lists seven sacred assemblies. One is weekly; the others are annual. One is a fast; five are festivals, including sacrificial meals where worshippers eat the sacrifices. Here are seven found in Lev 23:

- **Sabbath:** a weekly gathering (23:3) that celebrates both God's work in creation (Exod 20:11) and Israel's liberation from bondage (Deut 5:15). This was every Saturday, as we would call it today.

- **Passover:** an annual festival (23:4-8), which includes the opening festive meal and concludes a week later ("feast of the unleavened bread," Exod 12:17; 23:15; Deut 16:16) after a week of feasting. It remembers and celebrates liberation from enslavement in Egypt. This occurs in March or April.

- **Feast of First fruits** (23:9-14): an annual festival where Israel presents God with the first fruits of the harvest. God owns the land, and Israel acknowledges God's ownership and gifts by offering God their first fruits and rededicating their lives to God. This occurs the day after the Feast of Unleavened Bread concludes in March or April.

- **Feast of Weeks** (23:15-22; known as Pentecost in the Acts 2:1): an annual festival that included dedicatory and thanksgiving offerings for God as Israel celebrated the full harvest. This occurred in May or June.

- **The Feast of Trumpets** (23:23-25; Rosh Hashanah): an annual festival filled with joy and rest. This occurred in September or October.

- **The Fast of Atonement** (23:26-32; Yom Kippur): an annual fast day filled with mourning, lament, and confession of sin (cf. Lev 16). There was no feasting on this day. This occurred on the tenth day after the Feast of Trumpets.

- **The Feast of Booths** (23:33-44): an annual feast where Israel re-experienced the wilderness wandering through rest (no work), communal meals, and celebration. This occurred in later September or October after the Feast of Trumpets and the Day of Atonement.

While there are many themes that run through these sacred assemblies, I will briefly highlight four.

First, the number and regularity of sacred assemblies, mostly festive assemblies, is worth reflection. It seems God recognizes that human beings need rhythmic, regular, and frequent assemblies in order to integrate themselves into God's story. We not only need the constant reminders (you were liberated!) but practices that form and shape our identity and behavior. It is not simply the Hebrews as God's people who need this regularity; human beings need it.

Second, some, if not all, festivals testify to Israel's gratitude for and reliance upon God's regularity in creation. They ate together in festive meals. Israel celebrated the harvests in both the Fall and Spring. They also celebrated God's rest in creation through sabbath assemblies and the Feasts of Booths. They celebrated God's provision of land, food, and rest.

Third, they remembered their redemption. Whether it was their liberation from Egyptian enslavement or the forgiveness of sins, Israel gathered in sacred assembly to remember their history and embrace their story. They sought forgiveness through repentance and fasting, and they rejoiced in their deliverance through a week of feasting. Both were sacred assemblies before the Lord.

Fourth, except for the Day of Atonement which required fasting, the festivals included feasting, drinking, and celebrating. These were sacred assemblies. Though solemn and reverent, they were also festive. At the table (which the next chapter discusses), they rejoiced in their God and enjoyed the communion that comes through the table of the Lord. The meal, in fact, summed up the whole theological point: in gratitude and joy, Israel eats with God at the table upon which lies the animal that came from the altar. Festivals were sacred *and* festive.

Israel's Assemblies and Our Assemblies

Might we say that however Israel's assemblies served them, they might serve us as well in similar ways? Whatever God did through the assemblies of Israel, God can still do through assemblies today. We often focus on the discontinuities between ancient Israel and the contemporary church. Indeed, there are many. We no longer offer animal sacrifices, for example. Nevertheless, there is also continuity. Indeed, there is fulfillment. The assembly of the firstborn ones in Christ is not only continuous with the assemblies of Israel but the goal of God's redemptive work in the world itself. (We will discuss this in chapter eleven regarding Heb 12:18-22.) Given that continuity, in conclusion, let us stress some high points of this continuity.

When the church gathers as a community to praise, pray, and give thanks, is there a sense in which we "meet" God? The tent of meeting in Israel's story testifies to God's presence among the people. While God is present to all spaces, when God met Israel at the tent or temple, God was present in a redemptive way to commune with Israel. They assembled to meet God in a unique way. While some might think we no longer meet God in a unique way in Christ because we are indwelt by the Spirit and we are temples of the Holy Spirit, assembly is still a unique meeting-place as a corporate or communal practice. (We will have more to say about this in the coming chapters). This is part of the continuity between Israel and the Church. There is sacred space where we, as a community, meet God. When we gather to pray, remember, proclaim, give thanks, and sit at table, we continue the practices of Israel. The promises of God are still operative. Gentile believers have been grafted into the story of Israel, and that story includes regular and frequent assemblies where the people of God come before the face of God.

Just as Israel's story included a rhythm of assemblies that reminded Israel of their history with God and provided a means of encountering God to renew their covenant with God, the church also needs a similar sort of rhythm of regularity. This is not because we must reproduce what Israel did, but we must recognize the value of such regularity. As we discern what it meant for Israel, we can see what it might mean for the church as well. It is where we meet God in community with others. It is where we renew our covenant with God. It is where we commune with God as the body of Christ.

What is the value of a "calendar" in Israel's faith? How does this shape Israel? How does it remind Israel? Would a "calendar" also benefit Christians just as it did Israel?

God's invitation to Israel to regularly and frequently gather as a community contains a basic lesson for us. While we do not precisely reproduce their festivals, Christians have established ordinances or rituals that call for regularity and frequency. The community regularly baptizes, frequently assembles, and habitually gathers at the table of the Lord. Ritual is important for human beings. Families need it. It provides stability and identity. Regularity is formative. Without it, we lose continuity with our history and the story to which we belong. This is part of the significance of regular assemblies that express a rhythm of life. They form us over time; they give us stability and identity. Our gatherings proclaim the story of God. Our presence identifies us with that story and reminds us if we have forgotten. Assembly provides a way to remember, enjoy community, and encounter the living God.

While the primary act belongs to God who comes to us for our sake, we bring something to the assembly as well. Israel brought their first fruits, their sacrifices, and their thanksgivings. They confessed their faith and made vows before God. They worshiped and gave thanks in both lament and praise. As the church, we, too, bring something before God. We don't bring animal sacrifices, but we bring our own sacrificed lives to God in the assembly of the saints. Israel understood that as well. Psalm 40 reminds Israel that ultimately what God wants is not burnt offerings and sin offerings but the commitment to do the will of God (40:6-8). As living sacrifices, we come to the assembly bearing the gift of our lives as well as the gifts of our tongues in praise and thanksgiving (cf. Heb 13:15-16). We remember our vow in baptism, and we renew our covenant with God at the table. As such, the assembly serves essentially the same function in both Israel and in the church.

KEY IDEAS:

- The "day of assembly" at Mt. Sinai inaugurated the covenantal presence of God among Israel.
- Israel's assemblies were no mere rituals but communion with God.
- Israel's assemblies provided a rhythm that sustained Israel's life in the world and empowered their mission.

DISCIPLESHIP PROMPT:

Just as Israel was formed and shaped by their rhythmic habits of assembly, so disciples of Jesus are formed and shaped by theirs. God teaches us that regular rhythms of gathering together—whether in small groups or large assemblies—remind us of God's gracious history with us, become spaces where God encounters us, and provide moments of communal life. Assembly is not an addendum for disciples but lies at the root of life with God and God's people. For some specified amount of time (a month, six weeks, etc.), plan to meet a friend or two at a favorite place for a designated length of time, or meet via FaceTime, Zoom, Skype. During that time, decide to pray together, study a favorite book of the Bible, or even this book. Share with each other how your assembling together has impacted you.

PRAYER:

Our God, thank you for the invitation to enter your presence, feast on your love, and enjoy your communion. By the power of your Spirit, give us strength to embrace your invitation and share life with others who also seek your presence in the assembly. In the name of Jesus, Amen.

— 4 —

ISRAEL—EATING WITH GOD AT THE TABLE

Exodus 24:1-11; 2 Chronicles 30:21-27; Psalm 116

God eats with Israel in peace and communion.

"Consider the people of Israel," Paul wrote in 1 Cor 10:18, "are not those who eat the sacrifices participants in the altar?" Some are surprised to learn that Israel ate their sacrifices. We sometimes think sacrifices were burned up (one type was), or perhaps the carcasses with its meat were discarded as waste. After all, the most important thing about the sacrifice, we might think, is the death of the animal. What happens to the animal after that is seemingly irrelevant. However, as Paul remarks, Israel *ate* their sacrifices.

Whatever our misunderstanding might be, the sacrificial meals of Israel teach us something about the Lord's Supper in the church. Just as Israel participated in the altar when they ate and drank, so the church participates in the body and blood of Christ when we eat and drink (1 Cor 10:16). Ultimately, Israel ate and drank from the same source as disciples of Jesus do. Israel ate the "same spiritual food" and drank the "same spiritual drink" that believers do today, and that spiritual nourishment is Christ himself (1 Cor 10:3).

In the coming chapters we will explore in more detail the Lord's Table in the new covenant. In this chapter we will "consider," as Paul said, the sacrifices Israel ate and what it meant for them. This will, in turn, illuminate our own experience at the table today. We will begin at Exod 24, which was briefly noted in the previous chapter.

EXODUS 24:11

¹¹ *And [God] did not lay his hand on the chief men of the people of Israel; they behold God, and ate and drank.*

The Table on the Mountain

On "the day of the assembly," representatives of Israel ascended the holy mountain to eat with God. Before they climbed the mountain, Moses presented the people with a choice. He asked, will they obey the words of the covenant? The whole nation answered "with one voice, 'All the words that the Lord has spoken we will do'" (Exod 24:3). They committed themselves to covenantal obedience. As God's covenant people, they became God's "treasured possession," a "kingdom of priests and a holy nation" (Exod 19:5-6).

This commitment to the covenant was solemnized by two sacrifices and the sprinkling of blood. These two sacrifices are often associated with covenant-making or covenantal renewals: "burnt offerings" and "peace offerings" (Josh 8:31; 22:27-28; Judg 20:26; 2 Sam 24:25; 1 Kgs 9:25; 2 Chr 29:35) The first sacrifice expresses the dedication of the worshiper. The second testifies to peace and fellowship that exists between God and the worshiper.

The burnt offering is a dedicatory sacrifice. The whole animal is burned up since it is totally given to God. Greek translators rendered the Hebrew word as *holokautōma*, or holocaust. It is an expensive offering, especially considering the value of bulls in an agrarian economy. Worshipers keep nothing for themselves. It is all given to God; the worshiper does not eat anything from the animal. This represents the whole-hearted commitment of the worshiper. It symbolizes their dedication.

The peace offering is the other sacrifice offered in Exod 24. Its name is variously translated. Some call it a "fellowship" offering (NIV) and others a "well-being" offering (NRSV). Greek translators called it the "sacrifice of salvation." The Hebrew word is difficult to translate precisely, but it is filled with meaning. This offering establishes and practices peace (fellowship, well-being) between God and the worshiper. It is about the relationship between God and the worshiper. Where once, perhaps, there was no relationship or even a hostile one, now—through this offering—God initiates or renews relationship. The worshiper, through eating the offering, communes with God in peace.

This is why "the blood of the covenant" is sprinkled on both the altar and the people in Exod 24:6-8. This fuses the relationship between God and Israel. The blood sprinkled on the altar admits a sinful people into the presence of the holy God; it is purification or a cleansing. The blood sprinkled on the people solemnizes their commitment to obedience. The "blood of the covenant," we might say, makes peace between God and Israel so that they might sit at the same table together where Israel feasts in the presence of God.

The peace offering is particularly significant because it was practiced at all the festivals of Israel. Further, the peace offering is the primary sacrifice Israel ate. The fat of the animal is offered on the altar where the fire consumes it "as a food offering" to the Lord, and this gives off a "pleasing aroma" (Lev 3:16-17). The rest of the animal is distributed between the priests (specifically, the breast and right thigh) and the worshipers (Lev 7:11-18, 28-36). The animal becomes a food source for the families of the priests and worshipers, but the meal itself is sacred.

The meal celebrates the relationship between God and the people. Sometimes the peace offering is more specifically a thanksgiving offering (Lev 7:12), and sometimes it is a vow offering (Lev 7:16). Both involve a celebratory meal where worshipers invite the community to listen to their testimony (or vow) and eat with them. Sacrificial meals—eating the meat of sacrificed animals—was not a private moment. The meal was a communal event. The worshiper expected family and friends to celebrate with them as a community.

When the representatives of Israel ascended Mount Sinai on the day of the assembly, they entered holy space as people who had been sprinkled with the blood of animals. They "went up," Exod 24:9-10 says, "and they saw God." So we would not miss the significance of this phrase, the narrator repeats the theme in Exod 24:11 (though with a different word), "they beheld God." The Hebrew, as the translation suggests, uses two different Hebrew words. They saw God with their own eyes, as it were, and they gazed upon God as if in a prolonged vision. In other words, they experienced God and communed with God on the holy mountain as a redeemed and covenanted people. This was no fleeting moment but an intense communion between God and the representatives of Israel.

More specifically and especially significant for this chapter, they not only gazed in wonder upon God but also "ate and drank" (Exod 24:11). In effect, they sat at the offering table with God in peace and fellowship. They ate their peace offering sacrifices in the presence of God.

> How might Exod 24:1-11 inform our understanding of the Lord's Supper in our own context? What principles apply to our circumstances in the new covenant?

2 CHRONICLES 30.22b

22b *So they ate the food of the festival for seven days, sacrificing peace offerings and giving thanks to the LORD, the God of their fathers.*

The Fellowship Meal in Israel

The significance of the peace offering or fellowship meal in Israel is illustrated by the inauguration of the Levitical priesthood in Lev 9. Here Israel "drew near" to God in front of the tent of meeting and "stood before the Lord" (9:5). This drawing near and the subsequent ordination of the priesthood to represent Israel before God was enabled by a series of sacrifices: (1) sin offering for the priests, (2) burnt offering, (3) sin offering for the people, and (4) peace offering. After the series of sacrifices, God shows up as "the glory of the Lord appeared to all the people" and the people "fell on their faces" in awe and worship (9:23-24).

In the first movement, Aaron killed the sin offering for himself and his sons, sprinkled the blood, and poured it at the base of the altar to make atonement for their sins. Then, he killed the burnt offering and burned the whole animal on the altar as a symbol of their dedication to the Lord. Third, he slaughtered another sin offering for the people to make atonement for their sins. Lastly, he sacrificed the peace offerings, sprinkled the blood on the altar, burned the fat to God, and waved the breast and thigh reserved for the priests before the Lord.

The progression is important. Once the priestly sins are atoned, they can dedicate themselves to God through a burnt offering. Once the peoples' sins are atoned, they (though only the priests are named) can sit at table with God at a peace (fellowship) meal. The fellowship offering is the place where God and the people eat together. The animal is butchered and eaten. The meal is a concrete moment of fellowship. The table testifies to the peace that exists between God and the worshipers.

The peace offering, however, was not just for the priests. It was part of Israel's festivals. In fact, we may say the Passover itself was a type of peace offering, a thanksgiving meal for their deliverance from Egypt. Israel continually expressed their relationship with God through peace offerings. Through them Israel experienced renewal, peace, and fellowship with God. Moreover, this was not limited to the festivals. There were times in the lives of individuals where they offered peace offerings (thanksgivings, vows, etc.) and sat down to eat with God in the company of friends and families. We will see such an example in Psa 116 momentarily.

Nevertheless, the primary references to the peace offerings were the communal festivals or communal moments of covenant renewal. For example, when Israel entered the land, Moses commanded them to set up stones and an altar on Mount Ebal. Once they set up the altar, they were to offer burnt offerings to God and "sacrifice peace offerings," and then "eat there," and "rejoice before the LORD your God" (Deut 27:6-7; cf. Josh 8:30-35). Once in the land, they were to dedicate themselves anew to God and eat a fellowship meal with God. This illustrates the mood of peace offerings. They were not sad or somber moments but joyous ones. Moreover, this is not done in private but in community, and it is done before the face of God. In effect, God is present at the table when Israel eats a fellowship (peace) meal together. At that table, Israel "saw God."

Another example is Hezekiah's Passover in 2 Chr 30:21-27. This was such a joyous occasion that the leaders decided to extend the Passover week (the Feast of Unleavened Bread) an extra week. The celebration lasted two weeks instead of one. This meant that the "assembly" needed more animals, and the leaders supplied them: two thousand bulls and seventeen thousand sheep. Why are so many animals needed? Surely God can be satisfied with one or a few rather than thousands! But the truth is that they were celebrating with "peace offerings" as the people gave thanks to the God of Israel. Peace offerings meant they needed enough sacrifices to feed the "assembly" gathered in Jerusalem. "The whole assembly of Judah" along with "the whole assembly that came out of the land of Israel" as well as the "sojourners" in the land "rejoiced" as they celebrated God's salvation and deliverance. Their prayers, the Chronicler wrote, reached God's "holy habitation in heaven."

What we learn from Exod and the practice of the peace offering is that the altar is one thing, and the table is another. The blood is shed and sprinkled at the altar, but the sacrifice is consumed at the table. While the altar is an appropriate place for mourning and confession of sin, the table is the place of joy, communion, and peace with God. The two are deeply connected, of course. There is no table without an altar, but the altar is not the table. Because of the altar we are invited to eat with God at the table.

In your reading of the biblical texts for this lesson, how do you understand the distinction between the altar (where the animal is sacrificed) and the table (where the animal is eaten)? Is the Lord's Supper a table or an altar? What is the difference?

PSALM 116:12-14

¹² *More What shall I render to the* LORD
  for all his benefits to me?
¹³ *I will lift up the cup of salvation*
  And call on the name of the LORD,
¹⁴ *I will pay my vows to the* LORD
  In the presence of all his people.

Israel's Thanksgiving Meal and the Lord's Supper

Psalm 116 is a thanksgiving Psalm. "I love the Lord," the Psalmist says, "because he has heard my voice and my pleas for mercy" (116:1). The psalmist was entangled in the snares of death, on the cusp of death itself. Filling days and nights with cries for deliverance, the psalmist pleaded with God for help. And God delivered him from death.

In gratitude, the writer offers Psalm 116 as testimonial, a hymn of praise. The singer brings it to the temple, calls upon everyone to listen, and testifies to God's mercy. "What shall I render to the LORD for all his benefits to me?" the singer asks (Psa 116:12). How might he repay the Lord for God's goodness? Answer: there is nothing. No repayment is possible. Nevertheless, the psalmist knows how to respond (Psa 116:13-14, quoted under the heading above).

The "cup of salvation," we learn from the parallel in Psa 116:17, is part of the thanksgiving offering, a form of peace offering. The Psalmist expresses gratitude through offering a sacrifice which involves both food and drink. In other words, this servant of God can only repay with gratitude and dedication. He responds to God's mercy, which is God's own identity: "our God is merciful" (Psa 116:5).

From this psalm, we see at least three aspects of the thanksgiving meal (one kind of peace offering). First, the meal itself expresses gratitude and acknowledges God as the giver of all good gifts. Believers participate in a meal to declare that gratitude where they also can experience peace in God's presence because of God's salvation.

"Return, O my soul," the psalmist wrote, "to your rest; for the Lord has dealt bountifully with you" (Psa 116:7). Second, the psalmist remembers the vows made before God. The meal is a moment of renewal and recommitment. Those who sit at the table in a thanksgiving meal renew their vows and commit to keep them. Third, this meal is a public event. The psalmist gives thanks "in the presence of all his people." This thanksgiving and its renewed vows occur in the assembly of the Lord. In fact, it happens, according to Psa 116:19, in the temple, "the courts of the house of the LORD." The meal is a communal event.

What is the atmosphere and meaning of the fellowship meal in Israel? How might this shape our understanding and experience of the Lord's Supper?

The Lord's Supper is a thanksgiving meal. When Jesus took the bread, he gave thanks (Greek, *eucharisteō*) and broke it (Luke 22:19). This is why some followers of Jesus call this meal a Eucharist, which means thanksgiving. The Gospel of Mark uses both the language of blessing regarding the bread and thanksgiving regarding the cup (Mark 14:22-23). This is not a matter of blessing the bread but rather blessing God who gives the bread just as giving thanks for the cup is addressed to God. We bless God for God's gifts. We acknowledge these gifts are from God, and we give thanks for the body and blood of Jesus which was given for us for the forgiveness of our sins (Matt 26:27-28).

In the same context where Paul invited us to "consider" Israel's practice of eating the sacrifices, Paul offers a poignant reminder of the meaning of the Lord's Supper. It parallels the meaning of the peace offerings in Israel. When Israel ate the peace offering, they participated in the altar. They enjoyed the fellowship the altar made possible. The sprinkling of the blood at the altar—whether the stone altar at Mount Sinai or, in our setting, the cross of Jesus the Messiah—made peace between God and the people of God. The table, then, became the place of fellowship, peace, and thanksgiving. The table is the place where the people of God experience the joy and communion of God.

A CLOSER LOOK: "EUCHARIST" AND "THE LORD'S SUPPER"

As noted above, some followers of Jesus call the Lord's Supper the "Eucharist." This latter term comes from the Greek verb *eucharisteō*, which means "give thanks." The word "Eucharist" is not a translation of the Greek, but a transliteration, when one word is written using the closest approximate letters from another alphabet. This is similar to how the word "baptize" came into English: the Greek word *baptizō* (meaning "dip, immerse, plunge") was transliterated and became the English word "baptize." The Synoptic Gospels and Paul mention how Jesus gave thanks during the Last Supper (Mark 14:23; Matt 26:27; Luke 22:17; 1 Cor 10:24). Although some Christians may traditionally use one term or the other, both terms accurately reflect certain aspects of the same event.

In a similar way, the Lord's Table in the body of Christ is a place of thanksgiving, communion, and peace. This is the point of Paul's questions (1 Cor 10:16), "The cup of blessing that we bless, is it not a participation in the blood of Christ? The bread that we break, is it not a participation in the body of Christ?" It is similar to what Israel experienced but more. At the very least, the Lord's Table overflows with thanksgiving. It is a means of communion and fellowship with the altar (cross) and an experience of peace with God and other believers that the cross effects. It is a communal meal where the community gives thanks for the altar and enjoys peace.

In the light of Israel's practices, what would it mean to say the Lord's Supper is a covenant renewal meal? What connections to the Lord's Supper most moved you as you considered the sacrifices Israel ate?

Thanksgiving meals in Israel were always joyous and celebratory moments. Should not our Christian thanksgiving meal be the same?

KEY IDEAS:

- Israel's sacrificial ritual included eating the animal in God's presence.
- Given the altar and table practices of Israel, the Lord's Supper is a table, not an altar. The altar is the cross where the blood was shed, and the table is where we enjoy the peace the cross made possible.
- The table in Israel meant communion, relationship, peace, renewal, joy, and commitment.

DISCIPLESHIP PROMPT:

The table is both a joyous moment and a serious commitment. As a thanksgiving meal, the table enjoys peaceful communion with God. As a covenant meal, the table calls us to a committed life. We cannot serve two masters, and we cannot sit at two tables. We must choose between the table of the Lord and the table of other gods. As disciples of Jesus, when we sit at the Lord's Table, we give thanks for God's grace and renew our baptismal vows of allegiance to Jesus the Messiah. The table makes a claim on our lives. To eat and drink at the Lord's Table while living an intentionally double-minded life is to disrupt our peace with God and ultimately poison God's people. When you take the Lord's Supper, reflect on the sacrifice of Jesus and appreciate the joy of communing with God in this meal.

PRAYER:

Holy God, at your table, we ask how we might repay you for all your goodness? We confess we have nothing except to lift our cups and say, "Thank you!" You have invited us to your table to eat with you in your kingdom. Today, Father, at this table and in the power of the Spirit, we renew our commitment to you and vow to seek your will in all things. In Jesus's name, Amen!

– 5 –

JESUS—BAPTIZED WITH SINNERS IN THE JORDAN

Luke 3:1-22; Matthew 3:13-17

The baptism of Jesus is our baptism.

Israel consistently practiced their water rituals, regularly assembled as a community, and habitually ate sacrificial meals dedicated to the Lord. Yet, ultimately, Israel did not keep their vows and live out their covenantal commitments. As the prophet Amos tells it, Israel convicted the innocent, despised the poor, erected luxurious houses for themselves, practiced economic injustice, and embraced idolatry (Amos 5:4-13). As a result, God rejected their rituals and assemblies. "I hate, I despise your feasts!" the Lord said. "I take no delight in your solemn assemblies" (Amos 5:21). God no longer accepted their "burnt offerings" and "peace offerings" because they refused to "let justice roll down like waters, and righteousness like an ever-flowing stream" (Amos 5:22, 24).

Baptism, assembly, and table fellowship do not guarantee a healthy relationship with God. They testify to God's grace, invite us into God's presence, and summon us to a table of mercy, but they are meaningless if we don't seek God's righteousness (which is the priority, Matt 6:33). One cannot serve two masters, and one cannot in faithfulness simultaneously sit at the table of demons and at the Lord's Table (1 Cor 10:21).

Repentance is part of the process by which we approach God through baptism, assembly, and table. This is exactly where both the ministries of John the Baptizer and Jesus began. John proclaimed "a baptism of repentance" (Mark 1:4). Jesus announced the "gospel of God" by calling people to "repent and believe in the gospel" (Mark 1:14-15). As the gospel of the kingdom comes to Israel, its first word of grace is repentance and forgiveness. Israel's response to the gospel begins with repentance.

LUKE 3:2b-3

2b . . . *the word of God came to John the son of Zechariah in the wilderness.* 3 *And he went into all the region around the Jordan, proclaiming a baptism of repentance for the forgiveness of sins.*

The Baptism of John the Baptizer

In the fifteenth year of Tiberius Caesar, when Roman occupation oppressed the land of Israel, Jesus's cousin heard the call of God while he was in the wilderness. There John appeared as a prophet whose message prepared a path for the arrival of the Messiah. He became "a voice crying in the wilderness" to make Israel ready to receive their king, and through his reign "all flesh shall see the salvation of God" (Luke 4:1-6).

John preached in "all the region around the Jordan" and proclaimed "a baptism of repentance for the forgiveness of sins" (Luke 3:3). It seems like this baptism comes out of nowhere. It simply shows up as another aspect of John's peculiarity. After all, he did dress weirdly (camel hair) and ate strange things like locusts (Matt 3:4). Perhaps baptism is just another one of his idiosyncrasies. Such a conclusion, however, would ignore John's cultural world.

Ritual immersion in water was a daily practice in Israel during John's time. This pervasive practice was itself rooted in the Torah, as we saw in chapter three. Immersion in water or dipping oneself in water in a *mikveh* (essentially a baptistry) was a common custom in first century Judaism. Some people had them in the basement of their homes, and the Temple Mount in Jerusalem was surrounded by them. Priests, for example, would immerse themselves before entering the holy space of the Temple grounds. Consequently, John's baptismal practice would not have seemed strange to his audience.

At the same time, his practice was not without controversy. First, who authorized John to baptize others? It was not a question that those hostile to John wanted to answer because while they refused his baptism (Luke 7:28-30), they did not want to upset the crowd who believed John was a prophet (Matt 21:23-27). Indeed, it was the word of God that came to John; he received a prophetic call from God.

Second, his baptism demanded repentance and the confession of sin. This works at both communal and personal levels. John the prophet calls Israel to repent. Under Roman occupation their exile continues. They have not yet experienced the full restoration God promised in the prophets (for example, Joel 2:25-3:1). As Israel awaited God's redemptive work to restore Israel, they prayed, fasted, and repented as they yearned for the coming of the Messiah. John appears with a call to repentance because judgment is coming and "even now the ax is laid at the root of the trees" (Luke 3:9).

When the people heard about this coming judgment, John specified the meaning of repentance. For those who own too much, they should share what they have. For those who cheat others in their assessments, they should institute fair economic practices. For those who extort others and abuse their power, they should be content with their income (Luke 3:10-14). In other words, repentance entailed confessing one's sins and changing their habits, and Luke's account focuses on the economic sins of the people: they don't share, they cheat, and they abuse their power. Like Israel before the exile, the people are still engaged in sinful economic practices. As the kingdom of God arrives in the person of Jesus, they must change their practices, confess their sins, and renew their allegiance to God. Luke identifies this renewal with the "baptism of repentance for the forgiveness of sins" (Luke 3:3; cf. Matt 3:6).

Third, John baptized penitent believers "for the forgiveness of sins." Israel needs forgiveness both as an exiled nation and as individuals. Through the baptism of John, people reoriented their lives in allegiance to the coming Messiah as they confessed their sins and

61

received God's forgiveness. It was a renewal in anticipation of the restoration of Israel. In effect, John's baptism prepared people for the holy presence that was coming. As a penitent, forgiven people, they were ready for the appearance of the Messiah. John birthed, we might say, a remnant ready to receive the Messiah and participate in his reign.

> ## What are the emphases in the preaching and practices of John the Baptizer that prepare people to enter the kingdom of God?

Yet, it was only preparation. John only baptized in water in the light of repentance. His task was to reorient the people and cleanse a holy space in their hearts through forgiveness. But it was neither his prerogative nor within his power to baptize the people in the Holy Spirit. That must wait for the coming of the Messiah himself (Matt 3:11-12; Luke 3:16-17). John's mission, though the most important of all the prophets, was only preparatory. The Messiah himself will usher in the kingdom of God, not John (Matt 11:11-14; Luke 7:28).

LUKE 3:21-22

21 *Now when all the people were baptized, and when Jesus also had been baptized and was praying, the heavens opened,* 22 *and the Holy Spirit descended on him in bodily form, like a dove; and a voice came from heaven, "You are my beloved Son; with you I am well pleased."*

Jesus Is Baptized by John

At the end of a lengthy discussion of John's mission and baptismal practice, Luke in a rather matter-of-fact way concludes with the words quoted above (Luke 3:21-22). Jesus was baptized along with "all the people." The people came to John seeking the Messiah, confessing sin, and reorienting their lives to the coming kingdom of God through baptism. They submitted to a baptism designed for sinners, and they confessed their sins. It was designed as a "baptism of repentance for the forgiveness of sins" (Luke 3:4). And Jesus came to the same water the people did. But why did Jesus come? He was no sinner, and he had no sins to confess. Nevertheless, he was baptized by John.

The Gospel of Matthew explicitly raises this question. John objected to baptizing Jesus as he thought he needed Jesus's baptism rather than Jesus needing what he offered. John is a sinner; Jesus is not. But Jesus gives John a reason why he must be baptized like all others: "Let it be so now, for thus it is fitting for us to fulfill all righteousness" (Matthew 3:15). At bottom, according to Matthew, Jesus must obey God. It is the proper thing to do. To "fulfill all righteousness" is another way of describing obedience to the will of God. Righteousness is God's just demand upon human life; it is what is required. This is how Matthew uses the term in his gospel (see 5:10, 20; 6:1, 33). When we "fulfill" righteousness, we are doing the will of God.

At the same time, there is more happening here. "Righteousness" may have a fuller meaning in the sense of God's saving work. In other words, in this moment, Jesus takes up the Messianic role to lead the people of God. Perhaps Jesus is fulfilling the divine intent to redeem Israel from its sin and oppression by taking up the task of Messiah. He embraces the Messianic ministry in obedience to the will of the Father who sent him. Just as John "came to" Israel "in the way of righteousness" (Matt 21:32), now Jesus embraces this way as the righteous one, the holy one of Israel. The baptism of Jesus, then, is Jesus's own act of discipleship where he submits to the Father's kingdom agenda. Jesus professes allegiance through his baptism. He focuses his life on the ministry of the kingdom, which—we might say—is a kind of repentance. Jesus does not repent of evil, of course. Rather, he repents in the sense that he changes his life, turns toward his calling, and begins to pursue it.

In doing so, Jesus takes on the mantle of Israel as the true Israelite who will lead his people through a new Exodus into a new promised land. Both Matthew and Luke highlight the connection between Jesus and the story of Israel. In Jesus, Israel gets a "do-over" as Jesus recapitulates the story of Israel in his own life. Jesus relives the story to renew it and inaugurate a new age with the coming of the kingdom of God.

Israel	Jesus
Baptized in the Sea and Cloud	Baptized in the River Jordan
God Descends on the Tabernacle	Spirit Depends on Jesus
Forty Years in the Wilderness	Forty Days in the Wilderness
Entered the Promised Land	Entered Galilee for Ministry

As the representative of Israel, Jesus identifies with his people. He joins Israel in the water as a moment of solidarity with them. Jesus underwent a ritual designed for sinners. His humility and identification anticipate his willingness to suffer with Israel. Indeed, his baptism is his commitment to the way of the cross. Just as Jesus was numbered with the transgressors on the cross (Luke 22:37), so he is counted as part of penitent Israel in the water.

Why was Jesus baptized?
How is his baptism an example for us now?

The baptism of Jesus prefigures and entails his future suffering. Luke 12:50 uses the word baptism for his suffering: "I have a baptism to be baptized with, and how great is my distress until it is accomplished!" His baptism in water is his pledge to suffer for the kingdom of God. His wilderness experience tested this commitment. The devil tempted Jesus three times to exchange the way of the cross for more immediate rewards of food, power, and wealth (Luke 4:1-13). The Devil offered an alternative, but Jesus's allegiance was not shaken. Coming out of the wilderness, Jesus returned to Galilee "in the power of the Spirit" prepared to do the work of kingdom ministry. In this sense, Jesus embraced discipleship at his baptism and was discipled by the Spirit in the wilderness as one who would follow God's will in serving the world by giving up his life for the glory of God and in obedience to God.

Yet, we are a bit ahead of the story at this point. After his baptism, "Jesus, full of the Holy Spirit, returned from the Jordan and was led by the Spirit into the wilderness for forty days" (Luke 4:1-2). As Luke tells the story, the Holy Spirit both fills and leads Jesus. The Spirit will empower his ministry and fill him with joy (Luke 10:21). The Spirit is the presence of God which empowers, guides, and leads Jesus. God works through the Spirit within Jesus to usher in his kingdom, invading the present age which lies in the hands of the evil one and is ruled by evil powers. The Spirit is the presence and foretaste of the new, coming age. The Spirit is the presence of the future.

Jesus received this Spirit at his baptism when the Spirit descended on him in the form of a dove. To say the "heavens were opened" is to call attention to a special moment where God is acting in a redemptive way (cf. Isa 64:1). The dove may represent the end of judgment (like in the story of Noah, Gen 8:8-12). Perhaps it is allusion to the Spirit hovering over the waters of creation (Gen 1:2). The dove probably represents both. Nonetheless, something new and dramatic is at work here. It is the beginning of a new moment in history; it is the foretaste of new creation itself. The Spirit of God has descended to empower the ministry of Jesus, give life to his ministry, and to lead the Messiah in the completion of his task. Jesus has been anointed as the Messiah with power (Acts 10:38). In contrast to John's baptism, the baptism of Jesus is a pouring out of the Spirit. In this sense, the baptism of Jesus is the first Christian baptism, our baptism.

> **What does it mean to say that the baptism of Jesus is the "first Christian baptism"? How does the baptism of Jesus relate to our baptism?**

In this moment, like at Sinai, the voice of God bellows from God's dwelling place. "You are my beloved Son," God says, "with you I am well pleased" (Luke 3:21). The language echoes the Hebrew Bible. It is a combination of Isa 42:1 (perhaps also 62:4) and Psalm 2:7 ("my son"). In those Hebrew verses, God is addressing Israel or a representative of

65

Israel. In other words, Jesus is not addressed as someone other than Israel but as Israel's representative. Though it potentially harbors more meaning theologically (considering the virgin birth in Matthew 1), the language of sonship is primarily royal here. This is God's king whom God has chosen. This is God's Son whom God loves. This is God's Messiah in whom God delights. God affirms Jesus!

MATTHEW 3:15

15 *Jesus answered him, "Let it be so now, for thus it is fitting for us to fulfill all righteousness."*

Following Jesus into the Water

As the representative of Israel, Jesus began his journey at the water, just as Israel did. And this is where we begin our journey as well. As participants in the story of Israel, we join Israel and Jesus in the water. More specifically, we follow Jesus into the water. Just as Jesus obeyed God by entering the water, so we also obey God by being baptized.

Is this a sufficient reason for baptism: "I was baptized because Jesus was baptized, and I am a disciple of Jesus"?

Our baptism is a confession and repentance of our sins. As we stand at the water, we, too, hear the call of repentance, that is, to turn away from our sins and reorient our life in a new direction. We confess our sins, weep over them, and renounce evil, including the Devil whom Jesus rejected in the wilderness. Baptism, then, becomes a moment of turning. We turn from sin and false allegiances to a new allegiance.

Our baptism is a commitment to minister in the kingdom of God. Through the water we affirm our allegiance to the kingdom of God. We surrender our own agendas and commit to the agenda of the kingdom. Just as we followed Jesus into the water, so we come out of the water to follow Jesus in his ministry. Our baptism is an act of discipleship, not only in the sense that we followed Jesus into the water but also in the sense that we committed ourselves to follow Jesus and submit to his Lordship. Our baptism declares our allegiance.

Our baptism is a reception of the Holy Spirit who empowers our ministry in the kingdom of God. Just as Jesus was anointed with the Spirit in connection with his baptism, so we, too, are anointed with the Spirit in connection with our baptism. God not only anoints the Messiah but also his followers (cf. 2 Cor 1:21-22). Through this anointing, we commune with God through the indwelling Spirit, are daily transformed by the glorious work of the Spirit, and are gifted by the Spirit to serve in the kingdom of God with others and for others (cf. 1 Cor 3:16-17; 6:19-20; 12:3-7; 2 Cor 4:16; 6:16; 13:14).

Our baptism is a moment where God welcomes and affirms us. Though the words God speaks over Jesus may have some unique meaning, they are also words God spoke over Israel. I think they are words that are also for us since we are part of the story of Israel. When I baptize someone, I speak these words over them:

• *You are God's child!*
• *You are beloved by God!*
• *God is delighted with you!*

We carry these words with us for the rest of our lives. In our darkest moments, we can hear these words over and over in our memories. They are renewed when we witness the baptism of others. They are renewed when we assemble with other baptized believers and sit at the table with them. Our baptism is a marker of God's gracious invitation, reception, and inclusion. We have become part of Israel's story, and we, too, hear the words: "You are my beloved child with whom I am delighted!"

How does the baptism of Jesus shape our understanding of discipleship?

KEY IDEAS:

- The baptism of John prepared Israel for the kingdom of God.
- John baptized Jesus in water and God, by the Spirit, anointed him as the Messiah.
- Disciples of Jesus follow him into the water to participate in his Messianic ministry.

DISCIPLESHIP PROMPT:

Jesus joined Israel in the water and he invites us to follow him into the water. Joining Jesus in the water, we follow Jesus into the wilderness and participate in his ministry as his disciples. Baptism is an act of discipleship where we receive God's blessed anointing and commit ourselves to following Jesus, even to the cross. Baptism publicly marks the beginning of our journey with Jesus and constantly demands our allegiance. If you have not been baptized, will you consider it as you learn more about being Jesus's follower? If you have been baptized, continue to reflect on how your baptism is a participation in Israel's story of meeting God in water.

PRAYER:

God, confessing our sins, we have answered your invitation to join Jesus in the water, and we are grateful for your testimony at the water. Thank you for the grace you have poured out on us, especially the gifting of your Spirit. May we hear your call and wholeheartedly serve you in the power of the Spirit as we continue the ministry of Jesus in our lives and through the church. In the name of Jesus, Amen.

– 6 –

JESUS—PARTICIPANT IN AND FULFILLMENT OF THE ASSEMBLY

Luke 4:16; Matthew 18:19-20

> Jesus is the true temple of God by whom
> we worship the Father in the Spirit.

We may safely assume Joseph and Mary were good parents. This is evident in at least one significant respect (among many others, no doubt, that we do not know). According to Luke, Mary and Joseph "went to Jerusalem every year at the Feast of the Passover," and then tells a story about the time when "they went up according to custom" with their twelve-year-old son, Jesus (Luke 2:41-42). We might say that these parents discipled their son to attend the assemblies of God's people. It was part of their family culture, as much as we can discern from the record itself.

As we saw in chapter three, communal gatherings were important to Israel. They punctuated Israel's journey with God throughout each year. The sacred assemblies of Lev 23 served various purposes, but all of them were communal and focused on God's presence. In these assemblies, Israel encountered God in praise and prayer, professed their faith, and encouraged each other to continue their walk with God. There were assemblies for the atonement of sin, thanksgiving for God's harvests and blessings, joyful remembrances of God's deliverance, and embodiment of God's redemptive work in Israel's history. These were times of songs, prayers, teaching, thanksgiving, remembrance, testimony, eating and drinking together, and sharing resources. Through assembling, Israel renewed their relationship with God and each other.

Jesus, as the representative of Israel, did not abandon these assemblies, and he did not think they were superfluous or irrelevant. He participated in the sacred assemblies of Israel. As a devout Jew, he practiced the Torah traditions to both honor God and share life with God's people.

LUKE 4:16

16 And he came to Nazareth, where he had been brought up. And as was his custom, he went to the synagogue on the Sabbath day, and he stood up to read.

Jesus Went to "Church"

I am sometimes asked why I "go to church" rather than worship on my own in the glorious beauty of nature. There is no short answer to that question because "church" is variously understood. Church may mean "church building," or it could mean an "organized, institutionalized community" of some kind. But when I think about "church," I think about disciples of Jesus gathered for praise, prayer, and encouragement. I think about assembled disciples. So, the question is more, why do I gather with other disciples for praise, prayer, and encouragement? We may gather in a house, under a tree, on a mountain, in a dedicated sanctuary, or at the beach. We may be ten, or we may be a thousand. It does not matter where we gather or how many gather, the assembly—a community meeting as disciples of Jesus—is what matters. But why does it matter?

A CLOSER LOOK: "CHURCH"

In the New Testament, the word "church" translates the Greek word *ekklēsia* and occurs 114 times, mostly in Acts, Paul's letters, and Revelation. This term could refer to people gathered in a variety of assemblies, not just religious gatherings. The Greek translation of the Old Testament (called the Septuagint) frequently uses *ekklēsia* to refer to the gatherings of Israelites in solemn assembly (Deut 9:10 LXX; Josh 8:35 LXX). The word *ekklēsia* is a compound word formed by the Greek *ek* (out of, from) and *kaleō* (called, invited); although the New Testament authors do not make much of this etymology, it is not wrong to speak of the church as those who have been called out of sin, slavery, the world, and so on.[10]

In part, it matters because Jesus himself went to "church." I "go to church" because Jesus did. He assembled with other believers for praise, prayer, and encouragement. When Jesus arrived in Nazareth where he had been raised as a child, "he went to the synagogue on the Sabbath." This was nothing unusual because this "was his custom" (Luke 4:16). We might say Jesus went to church every week! It was his tradition, in the same way that the "custom of the Law" moved the parents of Jesus to bring him to the temple after his birth (Luke 2:27).

In addition, Jesus regularly attended the festivals of Israel. He not only attended local assemblies but gathered for regional and national assemblies as well. For example, in the Gospel of John, Jesus attended the following communal events within Israel's life with God:

- Passover (John 2:13)
- Unnamed Festival (perhaps Passover or Purim; John 5:1)
- Another Passover (John 6:1)
- Feast of Tabernacles (John 7:1)
- Feast of Dedication (John 10:22)
- Another Passover (John 12:1)

One of those is not even in the Torah, the Law of Moses. The Feast of Dedication or the Feast of Lights (Hanukkah) does not appear among the holy assemblies in Lev 23. It was started in response to some significant events surrounding the rededication of the temple in 139 BC. Thus, Jesus even participated in a festival that was not even

---

[10] For more, see the article by Graham H. Twelftree, "Church," *Dictionary of Jesus and the Gospels*, 2nd ed. (Downers Grove: InterVarsity, 2013), 138–42.

in his Bible, the Hebrew Scriptures. (And the synagogue is not in the Hebrew Bible either.)

Why was Jesus a habitual churchgoer? I can think of at least two reasons. On the one hand, he needed the opportunity as much as anyone. This is a good place to remember the authentic humanity of Jesus. As a human being, he needed the encouragement that comes from community. He sought community by attending the festivals and the regular assemblies of God's people.

Why did Jesus attend communal assemblies? How might his reasons encourage and disciple us about participating in assemblies?

On the other hand, he himself was the fulfillment of these festivals. He is the Passover lamb who takes away the sins of the world (John 1:29). At the Feast of Lights, he says, "I am the light of the world" (John 8:12). At the Passover, he says, "I am the bread of life" (John 6:35, 48). At the Feast of Tabernacles, he says that through faith in him, "living water" will flow from our hearts by the presence of the Spirit (John 7:38-39). Jesus participates in the festivals as one of God's people but also as the one in whom these festivals find their ultimate reality. The festivals teach us not only the story of God with Israel but also about our walk with God in Christ.

I imagine Jesus had many reasons to abandon these assemblies. Surely, they were filled with hypocrites and people hostile to his mission. The assemblies were by no means perfect in form or people. Nevertheless, Jesus still attended. There was something more important in that space than hypocrites and enemies. It was the space where God promised to encounter Israel as a community.

While hanging on the cross, Jesus lamented his death with a cry of dereliction, "My God, My God, why have you forsaken me?" (Matt 27:46). Jesus is quoting Psa 22:1. But Psa 22 does not end in lament. Rather, it ends with a victorious celebration of God's deliverance of the lamenter from death. In that thanksgiving, the psalmist sings, "I will tell of your name to my brothers; in the midst of the congregation I will praise you" (Psa 22:22). And these are also the words of Jesus in Heb 2:12. Jesus sings, even now, with his brothers and sisters in the midst of the congregation, the church or the assembly. Jesus still attends church.

So, when asked why I "go to church," my basic answer is because Jesus did. As a disciple of Jesus, I follow him into the assemblies of God's people. It is not only part of the tradition of Israel's sacred writings and the tradition of the Christian faith, but also prominent in the life and ministry of Jesus. If we are disciples of Jesus, we, too, will participate in the assemblies of God's people.

Why do you "go to church"?

We must be careful that we do not confuse the point. Some equate "worship" with assemblies as if disciples only worship when they are assembled. That is not what I mean. Our whole lives are an act of worship. We present ourselves to God daily as living sacrifices (Rom 12:1-2), and everything we do, we do to the glory of God (1 Cor 10:31). There is no dimension of life that is not dedicated to God and used for God's honor. We are always already worshiping. Israel knew this as well. While burnt offerings and sin offerings are important, what is more important is our desire to do the will of God. Israel offered their lives as the true sacrifices and, at the same time, told the story of deliverance "in the great congregation" (Psa 40:6-10). While worship is a bigger idea than assembly and encompasses all of life, when Israel assembled, they declared God's steadfast love and faithfulness through praise and prayer as a community in the great *ekklēsia* (church, assembly; Psa 40:9 LXX) or *synagōgē* (gathering; Psa 40:10 LXX).

Jesus himself embodied this reality. His life was a sacrifice as he went about doing good through his ministry which led to his sacrifice on the cross (Acts 10:38). His good works were sacrifices (Heb 13:15-16). At the same time, he proclaimed God's praise in the assemblies of Israel (Heb 2:12). It is a both/and; it is not an either/or. Jesus lived a sacrificial life that worshiped God with every breath and action, and he worshiped God in the assemblies of Israel.

MATTHEW 18:19-20

[19] *Again I say to you, if two of you agree on earth about anything they ask, it will be done for them by my Father in heaven.* [20] *For where two or three are gathered in my name, there am I among them.*

The Presence of Jesus

I do have another response to the question, why do I attend church? Another basic response—and I have many others which I will unfold later in this book—is, "Because Jesus is there." When the people of God assemble, Christ has promised his presence. Jesus still attends church.

In a real sense, Jesus is the church. Or, to put it more specifically, his body is the new temple of God. First, his own resurrected physical body is the temple of God (John 2:21). And, second, the church, as the body of Christ, is the new temple of God (Eph 1:22-23; 2:16-22). Jesus is the new temple of God, the sanctuary of worship, whether loving others in our daily lives or assembled as a community. We worship God through Jesus.

This is the point of John 4:24. It is a familiar text for many: "God is spirit, and those who worship him must worship in spirit and truth." Often this is understood to mean that we must worship God according to the truth of the Bible and with a good attitude or heart. But this does not fit well in the context. Jesus is contrasting the worship of Israel in the temple at Jerusalem with worshiping God "in spirit and truth." The contrast is not between truth and falsehood or a humble spirit and a prideful one. Rather, the contrast is between the fullness of "truth and spirit" and what was partial or anticipatory.

This contrast is part of John's teaching in the Gospel. It is a contrast between Moses and Jesus. This is not a matter of Jesus is good and Moses is bad. On the contrary, Moses is good, but Jesus is the fullness. Moses pointed toward Jesus and the fulfillment of Israel's worship and history in the Messiah. Jesus is the reality, or the Truth! At the temple, Israel worshiped according to regulations and with a good heart. In that sense, they worship "in truth and spirit" (2 Chr 31:21; cf. Josh 24:14). Jesus is describing something else. In the coming age, the new age of the kingdom of God, worshipers will seek God and worship in "Spirit and Truth."

Gospel of John	Moses	Jesus
1:17	Law	Grace and Truth
6:35	Manna in the Desert	Bread of Life
7:38	Water in the Desert	Living Water
8:12	Light in the Desert	Light of the World
2:21	Jerusalem Temple	New Temple
4:23-24	"in Jerusalem"	"in Spirit and in Truth"

In other words, these worshippers will not find "spirit and truth" in the Jerusalem temple in the way Jesus means it. They were already worshiping according to divine directive and with sincere hearts at the Jerusalem temple. Instead, they will find the Truth of God in Jesus who is the truth (John 14:6), and they will experience God in the Spirit of God. The Truth is Jesus himself, and the Spirit is the Holy Spirit (like elsewhere in the Gospel of John, 1:32; 3:5-6; 3:34; cf. 6:63; 7:38-39). The festivals of Israel will find their ultimate fulfillment in the person of Jesus and the work of the Spirit who enables those who seek to worship God to encounter the Father in Jesus and by the Spirit.

We no longer worship on a literal mountain (Sinai or Zion) but in the Spirit who energizes our souls and gives us access to the new temple of God who is Jesus. By the Spirit, we enter God's sanctuary, which is the Truth—Jesus himself. The time has arrived where we now worship God in the new temple (Jesus) by God's Holy Spirit.

How does this interpretation of John 4:24 differ from traditional understanding? Is it a both/and or an either/or?

Paul says something quite similar in Eph 2:18, "For through him [Christ] we both [Jew and Gentile] have access in one Spirit to the Father." Or, to put it another way, in the Holy Spirit, who unites us with God and each other, we know the bold freedom to share life with the Father because of what the Son has done for us in destroying the walls that separated us from each other and from the fullness of God's life. God has erected a new temple through Jesus, and the Spirit of God dwells in this temple to make it a "dwelling place for God" (Eph 2:21-22). Within this new temple, we boldly approach the Father through the Son in the power of the Spirit! Thus, we worship in Spirit and in Truth, and this is true both for our daily lives and for our assemblies.

How does this understanding of John 4:24 not only shape our understanding of assembly but also our understanding of life as worship?

Jesus, then, is always at church! It is his body. At the same time, Jesus is also present in a distinctive way when God's people are assembled. The Messiah promised his presence among disciples gathered to pray in a way that is not promised to disciples gathered at a baseball game. Truly, Christ is always present among disciples, whether assembled to pray or to watch a baseball game. Yet, there is a specific and profound promise to disciples who are gathered to pray (or praise God together). That promise is found in Matt 18:19-20.

While Matthew 18:15-20 is focused on a reconciliation process, it is also about assembly. In fact, the final part of the reconciliation process is to "tell it to the church" (assembly; *ekklēsia*). The assembly is part of the process itself. But what grounds the role of the assembly?

76

In Matt 18:19-20, Jesus provides the answer. He articulates a principle that is important not only for a reconciliation process but is significant for the assemblies in general. Jesus is describing an assembly, a gathering. The Greek word for "gathered" is a verb form of the noun we know in English as "synagogue." When even two or three gather, it constitutes an assembly in the sense Jesus is describing here.

At the same time, this gathering is both intentional and focused. The two or three (or however many) gather to pray. Also, they gather in the name of Jesus. More specifically, they gather into (*eis*, not *en* [see the discussion in chapter one above]) the name of Jesus: just as disciples are baptized into the name of the Father, Son, and Spirit (Matt 28:19-20), they also gather into the name of Jesus. In other words, they gather as people who belong to Jesus, or they gather as disciples who follow Jesus. When the disciples of Jesus gather, even if it is only two or three, they are an assembly to whom the Father listens when we pray.

Why does the Father answer such prayers? Matthew 18:20 provides the answer: because Jesus is present. The significance of this statement should not be underestimated. For example, the Midrash on Exodus 20:24 says, "Whenever ten persons assemble in a synagogue the Shekinah is with them, as it is said: 'God stands in the congregation of God' (Psa 82, 1)."[11] The Shekinah glory is the glory of God that dwells in the temple itself.

A CLOSER LOOK: MIDRASH

The term "Midrash" refers to any of a group of Jewish commentaries on the Hebrew Bible, written roughly between AD 400-1200. These commentaries, which are a combination of sermons, legal discussions, and meditations on the books of the Hebrew Bible, were written in Israel and Babylon by rabbis. Some Midrashim (plural of Midrash) are contained in the Babylonian

---

[11] For this quotation and more rabbinic sayings, see Joseph Sievers, "'Where Two or Three . . .': The Rabbinic Concept of Shekinah and Matthew 18:20," in *The Jewish Roots of Christian Liturgy*, ed. Eugene J. Fisher (New York: Paulist Press, 1990), 47-61.

Talmud, while others are found in independent collections of commentaries.[12]

How might the promise in Matt 18:20 give meaning to your experience of assemblies?

In effect, what Jesus promises is that whenever and wherever his disciples gather to pray and they gather as those who belong to him with the intention to follow him, Jesus is as present in that moment as the glory of God was present in the Temple. Jesus dwells in the midst of the congregation. He is present in the assembly as the mediator of prayer and praise who shines with the glory of resurrected life.

KEY IDEAS:

- As disciples of Jesus, we follow him into the assembly as participants in the gathered people of God.
- The Father seeks worshippers who will worship in Truth (Son of God) and in the (Holy) Spirit.
- When we assemble, we commune with the Father through the Son in the Spirit.
- When gathered as Jesus's disciples, Jesus is present to mediate our prayers and praise.

DISCIPLESHIP PROMPT:

Just as we followed Jesus into the water, so we follow Jesus into the assemblies of God's people. Since assembling with the community of faith was important for Jesus, it is important for his disciples. Jesus found value there, and as disciples we look for value there as well. Through assembling together, we are discipled into the life and story of

---

[12] "Midrash," in *Nelson's Illustrated Bible Dictionary*, ed. Herbert Lockyer, Sr. (Nashville: Thomas Nelson, 1986), 707.

God as we hear and enact that story together through song, prayer, reading, silence, sharing, listening, and communing at the table. If you are not part of a local body of God's people, seek out a community of faith with whom you can regularly assemble. If you already are a member of a local church, the next time you "go to church," reflect on the fact that you are doing something that Jesus did and valued.

PRAYER:

God, we come to you, our Father, through your Son in the power of your Spirit to give thanks for your blessings, affirm our allegiance, and petition for your grace. May our assemblies bring glory to your name throughout the whole earth as we lift up your Son as a light to the world through the strength and hope your Spirit gives us. In the name of Jesus, Amen!

– 7 –

JESUS—THE TABLE IN THE MINISTRY OF JESUS

Luke 5:27-32; 22:14-30

> Jesus hosts a table in his kingdom
> and eats with his disciples.

God has always sought to commune with humanity at tables. As we saw in chapter four, God sat at table with Israel when they ate their sacrifices, especially in the fellowship offerings. Then, God became flesh in the person of Jesus of Nazareth (John 1:1, 14), and Jesus sat at table with many diverse people during his ministry.

Those tables came in different spaces, forms, and occasions. The significance of the table in the ministry of Jesus has sometimes been undervalued and unrealized within the Christian community. It was integral to his ministry. For example, in the Gospel of Luke almost one-fifth of all the sentences in Luke's narrative are tied to a meal or table. It is where he did most of his teaching. It is no surprise that Jesus was constantly at tables, whether daily meals or communal festive meals. "The Son of Man," Jesus said, came "eating and drinking" (Luke 7:34). His ministry was a festive one!

The last table in the ministry of Jesus before his death was his supper with his disciples. It was a Passover table where Jesus and his disciples celebrated the story of Israel's liberation from Egypt together.

LUKE 5:30-32

[30] *And the Pharisees and their scribes grumbled at his disciples, saying, "Why do you eat and drink with tax collectors and sinners?"* [31] *And Jesus answered them, "Those who are well have no need of a physician, but those who are sick.* [32] *I have not come to call the righteous but sinners to repentance."*

Tables in the Ministry of Jesus: A Kingdom Etiquette

There is insufficient space to fully explore the table ministry of Jesus in the Gospel of Luke, which gives the most emphasis to table etiquette in the kingdom of God. The below chart follows the story of Luke through various tables. It is a representative list rather than an exhaustive one. It is sufficient, however, to see how pervasive the table theme and what sort of contexts and meanings are associated with each table narrative.

Text	Meal	Participants	Significance	Teaching Moment
5:27-32	Banquet at Levi's House	Tax Collectors and Sinners	Evangelism	"I have come to call not the righteous, but sinners to repentance."
7:36-50	Dinner at Simon the Pharisee's House	Pharisees, Guests, and the Sinful Woman	Reconciliation	"Your sins are forgiven."
9:10-17	Breaking Bread at Bethsaida	5000 Males	Mission/Service	"You give them something to eat."
10:38-42	Hospitality at the home of Martha	Disciples	Discipleship	"Mary has chosen the better part."

11:37-54	Noon Meal at a Pharisee's House	Pharisees and Teachers	Inner Life	"You Pharisees clean the outside of the cup, but inside you are full of greed and wickedness."
14:1-24	Sabbath dinner at a Pharisee's House	Pharisees and their Friends	Invitation to All	"When you give a banquet, invite the poor, the crippled, the lame, and the blind."
19:1-10	Hospitality at the home of Zacchaeus	Zacchaeus the Tax Collector and Others	Salvation for All	"The Son of Many came to seek and to save the lost."
22:7-38	The Last Supper—a Passover Meal	The Twelve, Including Judas	Thanksgiving	"Then he took a loaf of bread, and when he had given thanks, he broke it, and gave it to them."
24:13-35	Breaking Bread at Emmaus	Two Disciples	The Living One	Jesus was "made known to them in the breaking of the bread."
24:36-53	Supper with the Disciples	The Eleven and Others with Them	The Missionary Community	"You are witnesses of these things."

In light of the above chart, how does the table ministry of Jesus define or describe a kingdom table etiquette?

83

In the ministry of Jesus, the table is a place of evangelism, reconciliation, service, discipleship, spiritual formation, thanksgiving, and mission. It is part of the ministry of Jesus, and the table is a place where Jesus both rebukes and encourages, where he both challenges and embraces. One might say that at the center of the discipling ministry of Jesus is a shared table where he embodies the kingdom of God for the sake of others.

Jesus eats with the sinner as well as the righteous. He embraces the former and often rebukes the latter. Jesus invites the poor, the blind, and the lame to the table. Jesus ministers to the hungry, diseased, and lost at the table. The table of Jesus welcomes all and ministers to all. This reveals the kingdom etiquette for tables in the Christian community.

> **What does your table look like in your daily ministry of the kingdom? With whom do you eat? Is your table a missional one like the table of Jesus?**

LUKE 22:19b, 20b, 27, 29-30

19b *"This is my body, which is given for you. Do this in remembrance of me."*

20b *"This cup that is poured out for you is the new covenant in my blood."*

27 *"For who is greater, one who reclines at the table or one who serves? Is it not the one who reclines at the table? But I am among you as the one who serves."*

29 *"I assign to you, as my Father assigned to me, a kingdom, *30*that you may eat and drink at my table in my kingdom."*

The Last Table of Jesus Before His Death

The table ministry of Jesus is the background for understanding the Last Supper with his disciples. Every table in the Gospel of Luke bears witness to the kingdom of God as it models for us how we might hear and obey the good news of the kingdom. While it is one among many tables in the Gospel of Luke, the Last Supper, however, is a table where Jesus renews and extends the meaning of Israel's Passover as it is interpreted through the lens of his own sacrifice and life.

A Passover Meal

According to the Gospel of Luke, the last meal Jesus ate with his disciples before his death was a Passover meal (Luke 22:7-8, 15). Often, we tend to think of this moment as one of sadness and despair, but Jesus is talking about the coming of the kingdom of God. The expectation for the arrival of the Messianic kingdom is heightened at the time of Passover. Jesus does not squash those expectations but announces he would not eat or drink again with the disciples "until the kingdom of God comes" (Luke 22:18). This also makes sense of why the disciples argued with each other about who would be the greatest in the kingdom (Luke 22:24). They expected the kingdom to soon arrive, and they wondered who would sit at the right hand of King Jesus.

The Passover celebrates the liberation of Israel from Egyptian bondage. Its mood was one of joy, hope, and expectation. As it looked back to God's redemptive deliverance in the past, it also anticipated the future kingdom of God when Israel would be delivered from its exile (e.g., Roman occupation). It is a thanksgiving meal that celebrates liberation and anticipates further liberation.

> **What is a Passover meal? What is the mood and meaning of a Passover meal? How might our practice of the Lord's Supper continue the meaning of the Passover in light of the sacrifice of Jesus?**

Jesus begins the meal by announcing that the kingdom is coming and that the Passover meal itself will be fulfilled when he and the disciples eat together when the kingdom arrives (Luke 22:15-18). The Lord's Supper is not a totally new meal as if it came from nothing. Rather, it is a continuation of the Passover meal, perhaps even a continuation of all the sacrificial meals in Israel. At the same time, while there is continuity, there is also fulfillment. The meaning of the Passover—celebration of deliverance—receives its fullest meaning in the redemptive work that the Lord's Supper celebrates. As the fulfillment of the Passover, the Lord's Supper rejoices in God's deliverance from sin and all its consequences. It celebrates the arrival of the kingdom of God.

Jesus on the Table

I once heard that the table in our assemblies should be silent and somber because "the dead body of Jesus is on the table." I appreciate how this arises from thinking about Jesus as the sacrificial victim who gave his life for others. "This is my body which is given for you," or "This is my blood which is poured out for many." This connects the table to the cross since Jesus gave his body on the cross and poured his blood out on the cross. We eat the sacrificial victim just as Israel ate the Passover lamb and ate their thanksgiving sacrifices.

However, there is something amiss. Is it the "dead body of Jesus" on the table? I don't think so. Do we eat the dead body of Christ? I think not. For one thing, Jesus is not dead but alive, even at that moment Jesus offers the bread and fruit of the vine to his disciples. Are we nourished in the Supper by the dead body of Jesus or the living, resurrected body of Christ?

This is where John 6 is helpful. Jesus uses strong, even offensive, language that unless we eat his flesh and drink his blood, we will not have eternal life. In the context of John 6, the flesh and blood of Jesus are not understood as dead flesh and blood but as living nourishment. It is the living flesh and blood of Jesus that nourishes us. To eat the flesh of Jesus and to drink his blood is to intake life, an eternal life. It is to experience the life of the resurrected Jesus.

Resurrection language frames the teaching of Jesus in John 6. Whoever believes in the Son has eternal life, and "I will raise him up on the last day" (6:40). Jesus is the living bread of life, and those who eat and drink partake of life, eternal life.

Here is a way to visualize this. As we eat and drink, we are lifted into the presence of Christ by the power of the Holy Spirit. The Spirit takes us into the throne room of God to feed on Christ, that is, to be nourished by the power of his resurrected life. Through our physical eating and drinking, the Spirit pours life into us by virtue of the life-giving reality of Jesus Christ. In this way, the Supper is, as the second century martyr Ignatius long ago said, a "medicine of immortality" (Ign. *Eph.* 20:2). It is a means of grace by which God shares eternal life with us. It is the life of the resurrected Jesus.

When Jesus was raised from the dead, he ascended to the right hand of the Father. There he reigns as the resurrected Messiah, the first of the new creation. His humanity is now life-giving and through him all creation will be liberated and renewed. When we eat and drink, we participate in the new creation as we are nourished by new creation. Through eating his body and drinking his blood, we truly participate in that new creation ourselves as Christ nourishes us with his own life—a life-giving, eternal human body. This is accomplished through the Spirit by whom we participate in that new life. This is the meaning I attach to "This is my body" and "This is my blood," that is, it is an authentic communion with the resurrected life of Jesus. We are nourished by the body and blood of Jesus.

This feeding and drinking calls us to a new creation life even now. We are new creatures in Christ; we are empowered by his resurrected life. To eat and drink is to embrace the practice of new creation and the mission of God for his creation.

Jesus is on the table through the bread and the fruit of the vine. But it is not the dead body of Christ, but the living, resurrected new creation. The living Christ is on the table and offers life everlasting to his disciples. Jesus is "on" the table in the sense that the risen Christ nourishes us as one who already participates fully in the new creation. We eat the body of Christ and drink the blood of Christ at the Lord's table because the living Christ nourishes us through the Spirit which we receive as a gift from the Father.

Jesus at the Table

Jesus is the host of his table in the kingdom of God. The Living Christ is present at the table, seated with his guests, eating and drinking with them, welcoming them to the table, and providing the meal as a gracious gift.

Several key phrases in the Gospel accounts of the Last Supper reflect this idea. For example, Luke 22 announces Jesus's intent to eat the Passover and drink the fruit of the vine again when the meal finds its fulfillment in the kingdom of God (22:16-17). Jesus is no mere spectator at this meal, and neither is he merely the content of the meal (the Passover lamb). Rather, he is an active participant. He eats and drinks at the table.

More explicitly, in Matthew's account, Jesus expects that when he drinks the cup anew in the kingdom of God he will do so—as he says to his disciples—"*with you*" (26:29) just as earlier in the narrative Jesus had stated his intent "to keep the Passover . . . *with my disciples*" (26:18). This is significant language in Matthew as the evangelist begins his gospel with the coming of "Immanuel" which means "God with us" (1:23) and ends his gospel with the promise that the risen Lord would always be "with you" (28:20).

This language is pregnant with meaning. Christ is present. In whatever way Christ might be present through the bread and the fruit of the vine, Christ is also present as the host of the table itself. He takes the bread, blesses God, breaks it, and gives it to the disciples. He is both the lamb on the table as well as the host who provides the meal and guides it. Jesus is not a spectator but a participant.

The table is a shared meal—a mutuality, a reciprocity, an experience of active communion with the living Christ. At the table, Jesus hosts, eats and drinks, communes, shares, speaks, and loves. God is with us in the human, risen Christ at the table. We eat at God's kingdom table. We eat at the king's table.

This is a gracious gift and an expression of God's love. We—undeserving, unworthy—eat with God. We—unexpectedly, wondrously, joyfully—eat with Jesus. In such a light, why does sadness dominate our tables in the church? Why can we not eat and drink with joy since we eat and drink with the living Christ? Jesus is at the table! Why do we eat at the table on Sunday—resurrection day—like it is still Friday?

Jesus Serves the Table

Luke 22:24-30 is a fascinating text if for no other reason than that the disciples were arguing about who was the "greatest" in the kingdom while sitting at the same table with Jesus. Surely no believer has ever done that since!

But another reason this text fascinates me is that the instruction about service is also given by Matthew (20:20-28) and Mark (10:35-45) but at an entirely different moment in Jesus's life. Both use it as a response to the sons of Zebedee (and/or their mother!) who requested prominent places in the kingdom. Jesus responded by identifying the kind of royal service Jesus will provide. He will give his life as a ransom (Mark 10:45; Matthew 20:28). Luke puts a different but complementary spin on it. We can also imagine the disciples would argue about this on many occasions, much like we still do.

Luke places this saying of Jesus in the context of the last Passover Jesus observed with his disciples. While Matthew and Mark note that Jesus, unlike the kings and benefactors, serves others by dying for them, Luke notes that Jesus serves others by the way he conducts himself at the table. "For who is greater," Jesus says, "the one who is at the table or the one who serves? Is it not the one who is at the table? But I am among you as one who serves" (Luke 22:27).

Jesus waits on tables; he served the table of his disciples. Perhaps, if we bring John 13 into this, we can see this in the context of his washing of the disciples' feet. Or, perhaps, Luke means that Jesus served as a deacon (a word that sometimes meant "waiter" in the first century) in this moment. He waited on the disciples as they sat at table. Jesus is a servant because he waits on tables. Or, perhaps, the service Jesus provides is the gift of his body and blood which the table celebrates.

Perhaps Luke means all of the above. Whatever the case, the emphasis on servanthood is found earlier in Luke's Gospel. In Luke 12:33-40 Jesus tells a parable about a returning master for whom the servants are waiting. We might expect the parable to recount how when the master returned, the servants served him. But we get the opposite. When the master returned, the master himself prepared to serve, sat them at the table, and "wait[ed] on them" (12:37).

What a hopeful portrait! When Jesus returns, the reigning King will serve the community of faith at a table. The Messiah will be the waiter at his own banquet! The wonder of that thought draws me to praise and adoration as well as gratitude.

We might find comfort in recognizing that the incarnate God, the Messiah of Israel, embodied servanthood by waiting on tables. It is a surprising truth, even though we are so familiar with it that it does not shock us anymore. But to embrace the truth that the victorious king will serve his own banquet is a bit shocking even to us. It reveals the heart of God. God is a servant who creates and redeems for our sake. When Jesus waits on tables, it expresses the servant leadership that is part of God's own nature. God is a servant, and God calls us to serve just as Jesus served.

> **Which dimension of the Lord's Supper most resonates with your experience of the table— victim, host, or servant? Why?**

In summary, Jesus embodied servanthood at the table of the Last Supper with his disciples, which prefigures the reality of the Lord's Table in the kingdom of God. Jesus welcomes his disciples to the table as host, he serves the table like a waiter, and he offers his own life to eternally nourish our own lives. Jesus is host, servant, and nourishment.

KEY IDEAS:

- The table ministry of Jesus expresses and models a kingdom table etiquette.
- The last table Jesus shared with his disciples before his death was a Passover meal, which finds its fulfillment in the Lord's Supper.

• Jesus embodies servanthood at the table as host, servant, and nourishment.

DISCIPLESHIP PROMPT:

Like Jesus, we spend time at many tables: home, work, friends, and church. As disciples, we follow Jesus to the many kinds of tables. The ministry of Jesus calls us to serve people at these tables by introducing them to the kingdom and modeling kingdom etiquette at those tables. When we sit at the Lord's Table in an assembly of God's people, we commune with God and each other. Moreover, at that table God calls us to participate in the mission of Jesus. The table forms us into disciples of Jesus who became bread for the world so that we, too, might serve people as Jesus did. Jesus hosts us at the table, serves us there, and nourishes us so that we might become bread for the world. If you are studying this book as part of a Bible class or small group, find a church ministry or local nonprofit where you can serve together as a reminder of the way the Lord's Table prompts us toward service. If you are reading this book individually, reach out to other disciples of Jesus you know and make a plan to serve others with them.

PRAYER:

God, thank you for inviting us to your table where we are nourished and blessed. May we, Father, find solace and assurance at your table. May we also, Father, find strength and renewal to participate in your kingdom mission in the world. May this table express our unity so that we might serve the world as you have served us through your Son. In his name, Amen.

– 8 –

CHURCH—BAPTIZED IN WATER AND SPIRIT

Acts 2:16-17; 37-41; 10:44-48

> God initiates people into the assembly of
> the Lord through water and Spirit.

God sent John into the wilderness to prepare a people for the coming of the Messiah, baptizing them for the forgiveness of sins as they confessed and repented of their sins. Jesus was baptized by John as the Messiah joined Israel in the waters of commitment to the coming Kingdom. As the ministry of Jesus became more prominent than John (he must decrease and Jesus must increase, John 3:30), Jesus made and baptized "more disciples than John (although Jesus himself did not baptize, but only his disciples)" (John 4:1-2). After his resurrection, Jesus commissioned his disciples to "make disciples, baptizing them into the name of the Father, Son, and Holy Spirit" (Matt 28:19).

Baptism was no peripheral experiment. Rather, it was an integral part of making disciples in the ministries of John, Jesus, and the disciples. Consequently, we would expect it to have a significant place in the disciple-making practices of the early church. This is exactly what we find in the Book of Acts.

After his resurrection, Jesus spent forty days with his disciples teaching them "about the kingdom of God" (Acts 1:3). At the end of that time, he instructed them to remain in Jerusalem and wait for the "promise of the Father." This promise was their baptism in the Holy Spirit which God would pour out for the renewal of Israel (Acts

1:4-5). As they waited in Jerusalem, one hundred and twenty disciples of Jesus, including men and women, gathered to pray (Acts 1:14-15).

Were these disciples already baptized, either in the ministry of John or the ministry of Jesus? Neither the Gospels nor Acts explicitly say. However, Andrew and Philip were disciples of John. It is difficult to imagine they were not baptized. Moreover, Jesus himself was baptized and conducted a baptismal ministry. Would not his own disciples follow him into the water? It seems problematic to think that any of Jesus's own disciples were unbaptized. In fact, Jesus critiqued leaders who failed to submit to John's baptism (Luke 7:28-30). It is rather safe to assume that the disciples gathered in the upper room waiting for the promise of the Spirit were baptized people.

Yet, though baptized, they still lacked the presence of the Spirit. Jesus himself had been anointed with the Spirit at his baptism, but the disciples had not yet been baptized in the Spirit. That is what they are waiting for in Jerusalem. On the day of Pentecost, God poured out the Spirit upon them.

ACTS 2:17a

17a *But this is what was uttered through the prophet Joel: "And in the last days it shall be, God declares, that I will pour out my Spirit on all flesh."*

Pentecost: "What Does This Mean?"

On the day of Pentecost, the one hundred and twenty disciples gathered in the upper room became the core of a new community. As baptized disciples of Jesus, they received the Holy Spirit, like their Messiah, through an outpouring of God's presence. In other words, though this community had been baptized in water as disciples of John or Jesus, they were now baptized in the Spirit in accordance with the promise of the Father.

This promise predates the forty days Jesus spent with his disciples. It was promised by the prophet Joel (2:28-29). When the Spirit gave the disciples the ability to speak in tongues so that people from different nations heard the message of God in their own

94

language, a crowd gathered. The crowd was confused and amazed. They asked, "What does this mean?" (Acts 2:12).

Peter responded. It is not what you think, "but this is what was uttered through the prophet Joel" (Acts 2:16). What happened to the disciples was a sign of the restoration of Israel, a renewal of the people of God. It was the arrival of the "last days" when God would restore all things, and the pouring out of the Spirit was the effective sign of God's intent. It would include "all flesh" (Jew and Gentile), and it would include men and women, the enslaved and free, young and old (Acts 2:17-18). The effect of this outpouring is that "everyone who calls upon the name of the Lord will be saved" (Acts 2:21).

A new day had dawned. Just as God came to dwell with Israel at Mount Sinai in the tabernacle, now God comes to dwell through the Holy Spirit on Pentecost. This is the renewal of Israel for the sake of the nations, for the sake of "all flesh." The promised Holy Spirit is the effective sign of God's gracious intent which was secured by the death, resurrection, and enthronement of the Messiah (Acts 2:33). The Spirit testifies to the work of God in the Messiah, distributes gifts among the people of God, and is an empowering presence within renewed Israel.

This outpouring of the Spirit is so important that many have suggested the Acts of the Apostles should be titled the Acts of the Holy Spirit. Everyone who obeys God is given the Holy Spirit (Acts 5:32; 8:15). The Spirit fills the people of God for effective ministry and teaching (Acts 4:8; 6:10; 8:39), for prayer and communion (Acts 4:31), for comfort and joy (9:31; 13:52), and calls people into ministry and directs their service (13:2; 16:6-7; 19:21; 20:28). The Spirit is present to comfort with joy, transform people into the image of Christ, and empower ministry.

What is the significance of the pouring out of the Holy Spirit in Acts? Why is this an important point for the early church and for the rest of the book of Acts?

When talking about baptism in Acts, the Holy Spirit is often overlooked or devalued. But more is said about the Spirit in Acts than is said about water baptism. The Spirit comes upon a baptized people (with the exception of Cornelius), and the Spirit is present to transform and empower the people of God. The Spirit is the presence of the new age in the old age; it is the presence of the future kingdom of God. The pouring out of the Spirit in Acts 2 is the signal and means by which God renews and restores Israel through this new community of Christ-followers. The Spirit bears witness to God's redemptive presence in the world.

ACTS 2:37b-39

37b *"Brothers, what shall we do?* 38 *And Peter said to them, "Repent and be baptized everyone one of you in the name of Jesus Christ for the forgiveness of your sins, and you will receive the gift of the Holy Spirit.* 39 *For the promise is for you and for your children and for all who are far off, everyone whom the Lord our God calls to himself."*

Pentecost: "What Shall We Do?"

Convicted of rejecting the Messiah, Israel asked (as we ought as well), "What shall we do?" Peter's response in Acts 2:38 might have been spoken by John the Baptizer in Luke 3, but with a couple of significant differences.

The message is similar to John in calling everyone to repentance and baptism for the forgiveness of sins. Baptism was a moment of repentance and forgiveness, a new beginning in preparation for the coming Messiah. In this way, John invited Israel to renew their covenant with God in order to receive the Messiah. But this is where the similarities end.

In the light of Pentecost, where the enthroned Messiah poured out the Spirit upon his disciples, the renewal of Israel expands and deepens the meaning of baptism. First, it is baptism "in the name of Jesus Christ" or Jesus the Messiah. While being baptized "into the name of the Father, Son, and Holy Spirit" highlights the movement of people into the communion or community of the Triune God (Matt 28:19), "baptism in the name of Jesus Christ" is a commitment to the Lordship of the Messiah. It is an act of allegiance by which we confess Jesus is the Messiah and submit to the authority of his messianic Lordship.

Second, while John's baptism did not offer the Holy Spirit as a promised gift, baptism in the name of Jesus promises the gift of the Holy Spirit, which is the presence of the Holy Spirit. What Israel experienced at Sinai in the form of God's descent into the tabernacle, people baptized in the name of the Messiah experience as they receive God's presence through the indwelling of the Holy Spirit." The Holy Spirit is the gift; it is the promise of the Father (cf. Acts 10:44-45).

Third, Israel has waited for God's fulfillment of the promise to Abraham. Peter announces that this is that fulfillment, at least in part. The Spirit is the "promise of the Father" (Acts 1:4), the Father gives "the promise of the Holy Spirit" to Jesus who pours it out on his disciples (Acts 2:33), and the Spirit is promised to those who repent and are baptized (Acts 2:38). This promise is not only for those gathered in Jerusalem on Pentecost, but it also for their children and "for all who are far off" (Acts 2:39). While Peter may have thought only of the Jewish diaspora (until his encounter with Cornelius in Acts 10), it is clear from the rest of Acts that this promise includes the Gentiles or "all flesh." Renewed Israel, under the reign of King Jesus, welcomes uncircumcised but baptized Gentiles into the community of faith, and they also receive the promise of the Holy Spirit.

In response to God's exaltation of Jesus as both Lord and Messiah, we repent of our sins and submit to baptism in the name of Jesus for the forgiveness of sins. God promises to pour the Spirit upon all those who receive the message of the Gospel and obey it (Acts 5:32).

ACTS 10:46b-48a

46b *Then Peter declared,* 47 *"Can anyone withhold water for baptizing these people, who have received the Holy Spirit just as we have?"* 48 *And he commanded them to be baptized in the name of Jesus Christ.*

Conversion Narratives in Acts

Acts 2:38 was the first articulation of how people ought to respond to the exalted Messiah. This word in the inaugural sermon of the book and at the beginning of this new community functions as a norm in the book of Acts. On the day of Pentecost, the people heard the story of Jesus, believed Jesus was raised from the dead as the Davidic King (Messiah), repented of their sins, were baptized in the name of Jesus the Messiah, and received the gift of the promised Holy Spirit. These are the components we find in the rest of the story of Acts in one way or another.

> **How does Acts 2:38-39 serve a paradigmatic or normative function as we read the book of Acts? Why might we think this is the normative lens through which we read the rest of Acts?**

The conversion narratives recorded in Acts consistently highlight the following elements: hearing the good news of Jesus, believing it, repenting, being baptized, forgiveness of sins, and the gift of the Holy Spirit. The chart below identifies this consistency within the conversion narratives of Acts. I grew up with a form of this chart; so, this is not original with me. But it illustrates the general coherence of the conversion narratives in Acts.

Text	Heard	Believed	Repented	Immersed	Spirit	Result
Pentecost Acts 2:14-41	Heard 2:37	Believed 2:37	Repented 2:38	Immersed 2:41	At Immersion 2:38	Remission of Sins 2:38
Samaria Acts 8:5-13	Heard 8:12	Believed 8:13		Immersed 8:12-13	After Immersion 8:15-17	
Eunuch Acts 8:35-39	Heard 8:35	Believed 8:36		Immersed 8:38-39		Rejoicing 8:39

	Heard	Believed	Repented	Immersed	(Spirit)	(Result)
Saul Acts 9:1-18; 22:1-16	Heard 9:4-6	Believed 22:10	Repented 9:9	Immersed 9:18	At Immersion 9:17-18	Sins Washed Away 22:16
Cornelius Acts 10:34-48; 11:4-18; 15:9	Heard 10:44; 11:14	Believed 10:43	Repented 11:18	Immersed 10:48	Before Immersion 10:46-47	Purified Hearts 15:9
Lydia Acts 16:13-15	Heard 16:14	Believed 16:14		Immersed 16:15		
Jailer Acts 16:30-34	Heard 16:32	Believed 16:31	Repented 16:33	Immersed 16:33		Rejoiced 16:34
Corinthians Acts 18:8	Heard 18:8	Believed 18:8		Immersed 18:8		
Ephesian Disciples Acts 19:1-7	Heard 19:2	Believed 19:2		Immersed 19:5	After Immersion 19:6	

While the consistent elements are significant and need emphasis, it is also important to recognize the differences in these narratives. Not every element is specifically named in each conversion story, but that is not alarming or unusual. If Acts 2:38 functions as a norm, we might assume those normative elements in every story even if not specifically identified.

Nevertheless, one aspect is seemingly erratic. In the case of Cornelius, the "gift of the Spirit" is received before baptism. In the case of the Samaritans, the Spirit is received at some point much later than their baptism. But this supposed inconsistency is not as distressing as it might first appear. In both cases—Cornelius and the Samaritans—the narrator expands the conversion stories to explain the divergence from Acts 2:38.

It is important to remember the purpose of the narrator. Luke intended to tell the story of the growth of the church through the lens of its expansion from Jerusalem and Judea to Samaria and then to the ends of the earth (Acts 1:8). As the gospel comes to Samaria, the gift of the Holy Spirit is supplied through the laying on of the hands of the apostles sometime after their baptism. The entrance of Samaritans into the kingdom of God is confirmed by God giving the Spirit through the apostles. In the case of Cornelius (who represents the "ends of the earth" or uncircumcised Gentiles), the giving of the Spirit comes before baptism to secure their acceptance into the kingdom by circumcised Jewish disciples. In other words, the different scenarios are shaped by the different needs of the situation, which is to confirm the acceptance of Samaritans and Gentiles in the kingdom.

> **What is the relationship between the giving of the Spirit and baptism in water in the conversion narratives? Is there an "ordinary pattern" there? Why is there diversity?**

At the same time, one without the other is incomplete. Those who had the Spirit but were unbaptized were commanded to be baptized (Acts 10:48), and those who were baptized but did not have the Spirit were ultimately given the Spirit. No conversion narrative is complete until both baptism in water and baptism in the Holy Spirit are received.

Baptized in Water and Spirit

At this point, many raise a legitimate and important question. What is the relationship between the Holy Spirit and Baptism? What is the relationship between baptism in water and baptism in the Spirit? The conversion narratives of Acts closely connect them, and so do other texts in the New Testament.

- "[God] saved us, not because of works done by us in righteousness, but according to his own mercy, by the washing of regeneration and renewal of the Holy Spirit, whom he poured out on us richly through Jesus Christ our Savior" (Titus 3:5-6).

- Jesus answered, "Truly, truly, I say to you, unless one is born of water and the Spirit, he cannot enter the kingdom of God" (John 3:5).
- And such were some of you. But you were washed, you were sanctified, you were justified in the name of the Lord Jesus Christ and [in] the Spirit of our God (1 Cor 6:11).
- For in one Spirit we were all baptized into one body—Jews or Greeks, slaves or free—and all were made to drink of one Spirit (1 Cor 12:13).

These passages link water and the Spirit. We are saved through the bath of regeneration and renewal of the Spirit. We are born again of water and the Spirit. We were washed in the name of Jesus and in the Holy Spirit. We were baptized in the Spirit to become part of the one body of Christ.

While the exact relationship and mystery of this connection is not spelled out in any detail, the correlation of baptism and the Spirit is assumed. Just as the Spirit was poured out on the one hundred and twenty baptized disciples waiting in the upper room at Pentecost and three thousand baptized people received the gift of the Spirit, so those who are saved through the bath of regeneration and renewal of the Spirit have the Spirit poured out on them. Baptized believers are baptized in the Spirit, that is, the Spirit is poured out on them for the sake of communion, transformation, and empowerment.

This is not to say the water has any inherent efficacy. Rather, the water is an effective means of grace *because of* the Spirit's presence to effect the grace of baptism, including the forgiveness of sins. The water is part of God's good creation. It is a common grace in that sense, but the saving grace of water baptism comes through the work of the Spirit. At the same time, the Spirit is free to come and go as the Spirit pleases, like the wind (John 3:8). The case of Cornelius illustrates that freedom. He received the Spirit before his baptism in water. The work of the Spirit cannot be bound by our interpretations. It is wise to confess both the Spirit's freedom and God's promise of grace through baptism by the work of the Spirit. When we are baptized, we trust God's gracious promise, and those who claim to have the Spirit will seek baptism (just as Peter commanded Cornelius in Acts 10:48).

What is the function of the Spirit in our water baptism? What does the Spirit do?

The historic church has always surrounded baptism in water with various practices and symbols (including renouncing Satan and first communion after baptism). Others pray, sing, and testify, and some even throw a birthday party. Those are healthy practices that highlight the joyous nature of this divine act in our lives. Perhaps we might also seek to symbolize the coming of the Spirit in this moment as well. Our baptismal practice can also emphasize the coming of the Spirit as well as the forgiveness of sins.

The early church apparently used the "laying on of hands" as part of their baptismal practice. For some, this symbolized the bestowal of the Spirit. Hebrews 6:2 connects baptism and the laying on of the hands, which most probably is about the coming of the Spirit as in Acts 8. We might consider praying over the baptized person, laying our hands on them, and thanking God for opening the heavens to descend upon this newly baptized person in the person of the Holy Spirit. This is part of the grace God gives through baptism.

Baptism is a moment where God graces us with the forgiveness of sins and anoints us with the Holy Spirit (just as Jesus was anointed, Acts 10:38). At the same time, baptism is an act of discipleship whereby we proclaim our allegiance to the kingdom of God and commit ourselves to the mission of the Messiah.

How might we balance the presentation of baptism in water and the pouring out of the Spirit in our contemporary teaching and baptismal practices?

When we are baptized in water, God promises to baptize us in the Spirit. It is the gift of the Spirit, that is, the Spirit is a gift to God's people. The Messiah who invites us to follow him into the water baptizes us in the Spirit so that we, too, might receive the Holy Spirit and all the benefits and joys that come with the Spirit's presence. We follow Jesus into the water and receive from our Lord the gift of the Holy Spirit, just as he received the Spirit at his baptism. Filled with the Spirit, God leads us and empowers us in the Spirit to participate in the ministry of Jesus as disciples of Jesus!

KEY IDEAS:

- The conversion narratives in the Acts of the Apostles include both baptism in the name of Jesus and the gift of the Holy Spirit.
- God commands baptism as a means of grace to receive God's good gift of forgiveness and become part of the assembly of Jesus.
- God pours out the Holy Spirit upon believers who seek the will of God.

DISCIPLESHIP PROMPT:

In our baptism, we committed ourselves to God's purposes as an act of discipleship, and we received God's gifts. Our baptism is a constant reminder to continue to follow Jesus and participate in his ministry. We are gifted with the Spirit to pursue that mission and embody the life of Jesus in our lives. Let us remember our baptism and God's gift of the Spirit in our daily walk. We are forgiven and empowered disciples of Jesus.

PRAYER:

God, we remember our baptism today as the moment we committed ourselves to you and you graciously poured out your gifts upon us. Thank you for the grace of baptism and the presence of your Holy Spirit. May the power of your gifts shape our hearts and lives so that we might do your will in everything. In the name of Jesus, Amen.

– 9 –

CHURCH—ASSEMBLED AROUND WORD AND TABLE

Hebrews 12:18-24; Acts 2:42-47

Renewed Israel, like ancient Israel, practiced word and table in their assemblies.

Acts is Luke's second volume. In the first, he narrated "all that Jesus began to do and teach" (Acts 1:1). In the second volume, he describes how his disciples continued to do and teach what Jesus did and taught, both as individuals and local communities. While Jesus engaged in personal ministry among so many people in so many different ways, he also assembled with the people of Israel to pray and praise God, to hear the word of the Lord as well as teach it, and to eat the sacrifices at the table of the Lord. Jesus did what Israel did in its assemblies, and now his disciples continue to do what Jesus himself did as a faithful son in Israel.

God poured out the Spirit upon an assembly gathered to pray and wait for the coming of the kingdom. One hundred and twenty disciples of Jesus assembled on Mount Zion and received the gift of the Spirit. This one hundred and twenty were joined by three thousand newly baptized people on the day of Pentecost who also received the gift of the Spirit.

These disciples continued the ministry of Jesus whether as individuals in their own specific contexts or as assemblies of Jesus. In both ways, they are the presence of Jesus in the world to bear witness to the reign of God. What Jesus began to do and teach, this new community continued to do and teach. They taught the good news of the kingdom of God and practiced it. More specifically, they devoted themselves to the teaching of the apostles and to table fellowship, just like Israel devoted itself to the teaching of the Torah and sitting at fellowship tables eating the sacrifices.

Though I will give more attention to Luke 24 in the next chapter, in that chapter Luke previews his emphasis on word and table through the post-resurrection appearance of Jesus to two disciples. The two disciples met Jesus on the road to Emmaus. Their hearts burned within them as they heard how the Messiah must first suffer and then enter into glory. Their eyes were opened when Jesus was revealed as the living Messiah in the breaking of the bread. Those disciples practiced word and table that day, and the early church—following the path of Israel and its Messiah—continued the practice of word and table.

HEBREWS 12:18a, 22a

18a *For you have not come to what may be touched...* 22a *But you have come to Mount Zion and to the city of the living God, the heavenly Jerusalem.*

Mt. Sinai and Mt. Zion

The gathering of Israel at Mount Sinai on the day of assembly and the renewal of Israel at Mount Zion on Pentecost are deeply connected, though they are also different. Though Israel assembled on two different mountains, in both instances Israel received the word of God, experienced the descent of God, and ate at the table of God. Mount Zion is the renewal of God's relationship with Israel begun at Mount Sinai. The moments are parallel. At the same time, the Messiah is God's "Yes" to all the promises to Israel in the Hebrew Scriptures. Mount Zion is the fulfillment of Mount Sinai. God called Israel and dwelt among them, and now God calls all nations through the Messiah and dwells among them. The pouring of the Spirit through the Messiah is the fulfillment of the hopes of ancient Israel.

Mount Sinai (Ex 19, 24)	**Mount Zion** (Acts 2)
God inaugurates the covenant with Israel.	God renews relationship with Israel
God's presence is revealed through lightning and thunder.	God's presence is revealed by wind, fire, and tongues.
God came to dwell in the tabernacle.	God came to dwell in the hearts of renewed Israel.
God gave the law through Moses.	God taught Israel through the words uttered by the Spirit.
Israel gathered to hear the word of God.	Renewed Israel gathered to hear the teaching of the apostles.
Israel gathered to eat the sacrifices with God.	Renewed Israel gathered to break bread with Jesus.

On the day of assembly at Mount Sinai, God spoke to Israel (Exod 19:1-9) and Moses delivered the Torah, both in the form of the Ten Commandments (Exod 20:1-17) and the Book of the Covenant (Exod 21–23). On the mountain, Israel—represented by its leaders, priests, and seventy elders—ate and drank in the presence of God (Exod 24:9-11). That was the day Israel assembled before the Lord, heard the word of the Lord, and ate with God.

What is the continuity and discontinuity between Israel's experience of Israel at Mount Sinai and Israel's experience at Mount Zion?

Mount Zion is the renewal of that day at Mount Sinai. The pouring of the Spirit is the sign of the restoration of Israel (Joel 2:28-3:1). God does not descend through the Spirit to create a new people but to renew God's covenant people in order to bless all nations through the inclusion of the Gentiles. This renewal includes many of

107

the same practices. Specifically, it includes gathering the people of God for the practice of word and table.

The three thousand who were baptized assembled. They gathered in the temple to listen to the teaching of the apostles (Acts 5:42) and to pray. They gathered in homes in small groups to break bread at tables of praise and prayer. In Acts 2:42-47, renewed Israel essentially repeats what ancient Israel did in Exod 24:1-11. They assembled for word and table in the presence of God.

ACTS 2:42

42 *And they devoted themselves to the apostles' teaching and the fellowship, to the breaking of bread and the prayers.*

Devoted Disciples of Jesus

Acts 2:42 is a classic statement of the practices to which the early church was devoted. We might regard it as a succinct but programmatic summary for the rest of the book of Acts. The devoted commitment of the assembly in Jerusalem is a model for other disciples throughout the book of Acts. When disciples gathered, this is the sort of thing they did, though Acts 2:42 is neither a prescriptive nor exclusive pattern for assembling before the Lord.

Often interpreters enumerate these practices as four distinct items: (1) the teaching, (2) the fellowship, (3) the breaking of the bread, and (4) the prayers. That is possible, especially if "the fellowship" is identified with benevolence or the sharing of resources. Acts 2:44 suggests that understanding because the community held "all things in common (Greek: *koinos*)," which is a form of "fellowship (Greek: *koinōnia*)."

Nevertheless, the sentence's structure seems to suggest two categories: (1) the apostles teaching *and* (2) the fellowship. There is no "and" after fellowship which may indicate that the following two items (the breaking of the bread and the prayers) are expressions or forms of fellowship. It functions like a "that is" as in "fellowship, [that is,] the breaking of the bread and the prayers." Fellowship may include much more, like shared resources, since sharing with the poor is part of the fellowship of Jesus' community. Yet, the focus in Acts 2:42 is on the breaking of the bread and the prayers. In fact, the breaking of the bread, according to Acts 2:46, is shared food so that it is strongly connected with the idea of fellowship, that is, holding things in common (including food).

When they listened to the apostles' teaching in the temple, they gathered as a community. When they shared fellowship through breaking bread and prayers, they gathered as a community. Israel, in effect, assembled on Mt. Zion just as they had done at Mt. Sinai. The assembly of Israel is renewed as a Messianic assembly in whose name the three thousand had been baptized.

The disciples were devoted to the teaching of the apostles, the standard or norm for the church. This is teaching about the kingdom of God and Jesus the Messiah (Acts 1:3; 8:12; 19:8; 28:23, 31). They were with Jesus for forty days after his resurrection. Those were days when Jesus clarified his mission, spoke to them about the kingdom of God, and helped them read the Hebrew Scriptures in light of his own person and work. If we wonder what the teaching of the apostles looked like, we need only to read the sermons in Acts (e.g., Peter's sermon in Acts 3 or his summary to Cornelius in Acts 10). It was the story of Israel, Jesus, and the renewal of Israel.

When you hear the phrase "apostles' teaching," what sort of teaching do you think the phrase has in mind? What does it mean to teach about the kingdom of God?

While they gathered as a large community at the temple for teaching and prayers, they also gathered as smaller communities in homes for the breaking of bread. Their assemblies were not all the same sort of thing. Rather, they assembled in different ways in order to experience different dimensions of the reality of the Spirit. Perhaps thousands gathered in the temple to listen to the word and participate in the prayers of the temple, and they also gathered in small groups in homes to eat together as they continued their prayer and praise.

The disciples were devoted to *fellowship*. The term is a broad one that includes any kind of sharing, including the sharing of resources with each other. But Acts 2:42 identifies two ways in which this fellowship was expressed. The language of breaking of the bread comes from Luke 24:30, 35 (cf. Luke 9:16; 22:19) where Jesus is revealed in the breaking of the bread. This is the meal at which Jesus sits as host in his kingdom. Acts 20:7-12 is another occasion for the breaking of bread in the church (which is discussed in the next chapter; cf. 1 Cor 10:16 as well). As renewed Israel, they continued Israel's table practices, including the fulfillment of the Passover and thanksgiving meals. They ate together, and they ate in the presence of God, particularly in the presence of the living Jesus who hosts the table. It is a resurrection meal, for in the breaking of the bread Jesus is revealed (see the next chapter for more on this point).

When you hear the word "fellowship," what does that bring to mind? What was the content of the "fellowship" in Acts 2? How do you define and practice "fellowship" in your congregational life?

Some suggest that the breaking of bread in Acts 2:42 is different from the breaking of bread in Acts 2:46. The language of breaking bread is dependent upon the Gospel of Luke. There Luke identifies the breaking of bread with a meal hosted by Jesus (Luke 9:16; 22:19; 24:30, 35). This is part of the continuity between the ministry of Jesus and the practices of the early church. It seems rather odd that Luke would use the same language to describe two different things in the space of five verses (Acts 2:42 and 46), especially when the text is describing the same people, professing the same faith, in the same city, during the same time period, and continuing the same actions to which the community was devoted. Acts 2:42 says they devoted themselves to the breaking of the bread, and Acts 2:46 says they did it. To recognize that Acts 2:46 is describing a meal with food is to appreciate that Acts

2:42 refers to a similar meal as well (and so are Luke 9; 22; and 24). We will say more about the nature of the meal in chapter thirteen.

The second form of fellowship Luke identifies is "the prayers." Jerusalem was a praying church (cf. Acts 4:23-31; 12:12). The church continued the prayer life of Jesus's ministry as Jesus taught them to pray (Luke 11:1-12). The text refers to "the prayers." This probably refers to set times for prayer. Perhaps they even recited prayers as was typical among devout Jews who prayed at the temple (e.g., Peter and John go up to the temple for the prayers in Acts 3).

Acts 2:43-47 summarizes how the early church lived out Acts 2:42. The disciples gathered in the temple daily to hear the teaching of the apostles and, presumably, to pray together or participate in the daily temple prayers (like Peter and John did in Acts 3). The disciples shared their resources with each other as an expression of their fellowship, and they also gathered in their homes daily to break bread together. Their fellowship included not only sharing financial resources as they sold their possessions to give to the needy but sharing their food with each other. Sharing food is part of the fellowship of the assembly of Jesus.

Both of these activities—teaching and breaking bread—are characterized as "praising God," and they generated a good reputation in the community. The church grew. Practicing the kingdom of God through word and table honors God and builds relationships with the community and within the community of God.

The baptized community assembled to hear the word of the Lord, and they assembled to fellowship, which included the breaking of the bread and the prayers. This was a continuation of Israel's own life with God which began with a "day of assembly" and continued through the teaching of the law and eating at tables with God. The church, grafted into the tree of Israel, continues the similar practices: assembly, teaching, and table.

ACTS 2:46-47a

^{46} *And day by day, attending the temple together and breaking bread in their homes, they received their food with glad and generous hearts,* ^{47} *praising God and having favor with all the people.*

Assembly as Word and Table in the Spirit

While the function of Acts 2:42 encompasses more than assemblies, these practices are also intertwined with community. For example, teaching involves at least two (teacher and student) but typically involves more as Israel gathered in the temple as well as house to house to listen to the apostles (Acts 5:42). Fellowship assumes a community, and in this context eating is not a solitary event. These practices, in the context of Acts 2, are communal.

> How is the communal life of word and table experienced in your own congregational life? What emphases are present and what are missing?

They also take place in the Spirit. God poured out the Spirit on this community so that they are alive in the Spirit. Renewed Israel is filled with the Spirit (Acts 2:4; 4:8, 31; 6:3; 13:52). The descent of the Spirit, like the descent of God into the tabernacle, means that we encounter God not only in our personal experiences but also in communal spaces, especially when the community assembles. The Spirit fills the assembly (Acts 4:31), directs it, and empowers it. When we assemble, God is present and active. We worship in the Spirit (John 4:24; Phil 3:3).

God's presence in the assembly by the Spirit means God is active. When the word of God is preached or taught, God accompanies that word with God's own power. The word is no mere cognitive persuasion but the work of the Spirit who uses the word to accomplish God's purposes (Isa 55:8-11). The Word of God is the sword of the Spirit (Eph 6:17; praying "in the Spirit" is also another weapon, Eph 6:18). The proclamation of the gospel in the assembly of the Lord is empowered by the work of the Spirit because the word of God comes to us "not only in word, but also in power and in the Holy Spirit" (1 Thess 1:5). Through the word and in the power of the Spirit, God convicts us, and comforts us by the love of God in Christ Jesus. We receive the faithful preaching of the gospel as God's word to us by which the Spirit works in our hearts for our sanctification (2 Thess 2:13).

God is also active at the table of the Lord. The tendency is to think of the table as something we do: we remember, we eat, we drink, and we give thanks. And we certainly do. But we might also ask, what is God doing at the table? What is the Spirit of God, who fills us and sanctifies, doing at the table? In the breaking of the bread the living presence of the Messiah who hosts the table is revealed. How is the Messiah present? Though that question has been debated in many ways, perhaps we can at least say that the Messiah is present through the Spirit. The exalted Messiah, who sits at the right of God, is connected to us by the Spirit when we eat the bread and drink the fruit of the vine. We eat and drink at the table of Jesus who hosts the table as the resurrected Lord. He hosts that table through the Spirit.

How does the table embody the word and how does the word interpret the table? How do they give meaning to each other?

In the Spirit, we announce the gospel by preaching the word, and we embody the gospel through eating and drinking at the table of the Lord. The gospel proclaims the meaning of the table, and the table is the experience of the gospel. The two go together: word and table. This happens when the people of God assemble. We listen to the preaching of the gospel to understand the table, and we eat and drink at the table to experience the gospel. Together, in the Spirit, we encounter the living Messiah in word and deed through the preached gospel and the hosted table.

113

KEY IDEAS:

- The early church continued the practices of both ancient Israel and the ministry of Jesus in their assemblies.
- This new community of disciples gathered daily to learn from the teaching of the apostles and participate in the prayers of the people.
- The new community gathered daily to break bread in homes with joy and devotion.

DISCIPLESHIP PROMPT:

The first disciples of Jesus after Pentecost devoted themselves to the teaching of the apostles and the fellowship of the breaking the bread and the prayers. Just as we followed Jesus into the water, so we also continue the practice of assembling for word and table. Constant devotion to word and table in the assemblies of Jesus forms disciples into the image of Christ by guiding their decisions through teaching and empowering their lives through communing with the living Christ at the table. Disciples are formed in community rather than in isolation. Consequently, just like Jesus, we participate in the assemblies of the Lord through word and table. When you reflect on this, do you find yourself preferring or prioritizing one over the other? The next time you assemble with God's people, reflect on how both of these practices help to form us as disciples of Jesus.

PRAYER:

God, fill our hearts with the same devotion modeled by your people in Jerusalem in the days following Pentecost. May our assemblies listen to the apostolic teaching and break bread together in joy and commitment. Give us eyes to see your work within our assemblies by the presence of your Spirit as we honor and praise your name together. In the name of Jesus, Amen.

CHURCH—EATING WITH JESUS AT TABLE

Luke 24:13-35; Acts 20:7-12; Revelation 1:10, 17-18

> The living Jesus hosts the table in the
> assembly of renewed Israel.

When three thousand people gladly received the good news about the resurrection and enthronement of Jesus the Messiah on the day of Pentecost, they were baptized in his name for the forgiveness of sins and received the gift of the Holy Spirit. They were added to the one hundred and twenty to form the nucleus of a renewed assembly of Israel to spread the news of God's saving work through Jesus in the Spirit (Acts 2:38-41).

This community "devoted themselves to the apostles' teaching and the fellowship, to the breaking of bread and the prayers" (Acts 2:42). What does devotion to "the breaking of bread" mean? That phrase appears without any explanation. Yet, it is so important that these disciples of Jesus persevered in that practice. Just as they were devoted to prayer in Acts 1:14, so now they are devoted to these practices, including the breaking of bread.

If we may judge from the importance of the "apostles' teaching," which provided a norm and guide for these disciples, the breaking of bread was also a significant aspect of their life together. It was part of their shared life, their fellowship. The verb "devoted" is the same word as in Acts 2:46 where the disciples continually gathered in the temple and broke bread in their homes. They were devoted to assembling in the temple to hear the teaching of the apostles every day and gathering in homes to break bread every day. The breaking of bread, like listening to the teaching of the apostles, was a foundational practice for the Jerusalem church.

From Acts 2:46-47, we learn this breaking of bread (1) was a meal where they consumed food, (2) it was a form of benevolent fellowship as they generously shared their food, (3) they engaged in the praise of God, and (4) the gathering was filled with joy. The breaking of bread in Acts 2:46 was a daily supper of generous hospitality overflowing with joy and praise. Acts 2:42 states the disciples were devoted to breaking bread, and Acts 2:46 says they devoutly continued to meet together in the temple and breaking of bread at home. The church gathered, we might say, as thousands at the temple for teaching and prayer, but they also gathered in small groups in homes to break bread together.

But exactly what is the breaking of the bread? Though Luke does not explain it in Acts 2, he does not leave us clueless. We must read the beginning of the story as well as the rest of the story.

LUKE 24:30-31a, 35

30 When he was at table with them, he took the bread and blessed and broke it and gave it to them. 31 And their eyes were opened, and they recognized him… 35 Then they told what had happened on the road, and how he was known to them in the breaking of the bread.

Their Eyes Were Opened

The beginning of the story is Jesus. He broke bread with his followers in the Gospel of Luke. We must read and understand the first volume of Luke's history in order to understand his puzzling reference to breaking bread in Acts 2:42. Luke assumes his readers know what it means because they have read the first volume of his history where he describes it.

Perhaps an illustration would help. Suppose you are reading or watching the movie *The Return of the King* in *The Lord of the Rings* trilogy. You notice repeated references to the Shire without any further

116

information. The writer or director simply assumes you know what the Shire is and its meaning in the story. This is assumed because the Shire was fully explored in the first volume, *The Fellowship of the Ring* or in a previous book, *The Hobbit*. The writer or director does not have to repeatedly explain what the Shire is because readers or viewers should already know what it is from previous story-telling.

The Gospel of Luke, the volume previous to Acts in Luke's histories, uses the language of breaking bread in three accounts (Luke 9:16; 22:19; 24:30, 35). The first is the feeding of the five thousand where Jesus, as the Messiah, feeds his people in the wilderness. The second is at the Last Supper with his disciples. The third is in the home of the two disciples whom Jesus joined on their journey from Jerusalem to Emmaus. In each account, Jesus (1) takes the bread, (2) gives thanks to God or blesses God, (3) breaks the bread, and (4) gives it or distributes it. This four-fold action is repeated in each text. Some see a liturgical pattern here: we take the bread, give thanks, break it, and give it to each other.

Luke	Meaning	Acts
Luke 9:16: Jesus took bread, blessed, broke and gave it.		*Acts 2:42:* the disciples continued in the breaking of bread.
Luke 22:19: Jesus took bread, gave thanks, broke, and gave it.	*Luke 24:35:* Jesus was "made known to them in the breaking of the bread."	*Acts 2:46:* the disciples broke bread daily in their homes.
Luke 24:30: Jesus took bread, blessed, broke, and gave it.		*Acts 20:7:* the disciples gathered to break bread.

But what is the meaning of this thematic thread in the Gospel of Luke? The common elements include:

• It is a meal where food is consumed.

• The Messiah hosts the meal.

117

- The meal is a communal event, whether five thousand, thirteen, or three.
- The host gives thanks to or blesses God.
- The meal provides and proclaims life.
- Everyone eats.

More particularly, Luke provides an interpretative window for the meal in the post-resurrection story in Luke 24:13-35.

On the first day of the week, the women found the tomb of Jesus empty. Two men, appearing in dazzling robes, announced to the women, "He is not here, but has risen." The women immediately went "to the eleven and to all the rest" to tell the good news that the Lord is risen. "But these words seemed to them like an idle tale, and they did not believe them." Two of these disciples, Cleopas and perhaps his wife, began to walk to their home in Emmaus seven miles from Jerusalem. They were discouraged, hopeless, and perplexed by the story the women told. Even though it was Sunday, the first day of the week, it was still Friday in their spirits. They were still living in the grief and disappointment of Friday.

Jesus joined their conversation incognito as "their eyes were kept from recognizing him" by God. He listened, and then he began to explain how the Messiah must first suffer and then enter into glory. "And beginning with Moses and all the Prophets, he interpreted to them in all the Scriptures the things concerning himself." Yet, Cleopas and his wife still did not recognize him. Nevertheless, their hearts burned within them as they listened to his explanation of the Scriptures.

As the group drew near to their home in Emmaus, they invited Jesus to stay the evening. Their hospitality, of course, included a meal. As they reclined at the table, Jesus assumed the role of host even though he was the guest! He took the bread, blessed God, broke it, and gave it to the two disciples, just as Jesus did at the Last Supper in Luke 22:16. Remember that Jesus said he would not eat or drink with them again until the kingdom of God had come, but here Jesus is eating and drinking with them at a meal in the kingdom of God. The kingdom had come, in some sense, in the resurrection of Jesus. This becomes immediately apparent to the two disciples.

Though their eyes were prevented from recognizing Jesus on the road to Emmaus, now "their eyes were opened, and they recognized him." At the table, the disciples encountered the living Messiah. Earlier that Sunday afternoon their hearts were still burdened with the despair of Friday because they "had hoped" Jesus was the Messiah. But now their mourning is transformed into rejoicing, their despair into hope, and death into life. The table was transformative. It reoriented the disciples because at the table they encountered the living Messiah.

Excited, the disciples immediately returned to Jerusalem where they met with other disciples that evening. The women were saying, "He is risen." The disciples in Jerusalem were also now saying, "The Lord has risen indeed." And the two disciples from Emmaus add how "he was known to them in the breaking of the bread."

We might say their experience at the table was an epiphany; it was a moment when their eyes were opened. They could see something that they could not see previously. They experienced a truth that they had not previously known. They encountered the living Messiah at the table in the breaking of the bread. Jesus was revealed to them at the table.

> **How should the resurrection function in our understanding of the meaning of the Lord's Supper? Why do we tend to concentrate more on the victim (death) character of the Supper than we do the host (resurrection) dimension of the Supper?**

The journey to Emmaus is a journey of word (Scripture) and table (breaking bread). Jesus interpreted and explained the Scriptures to them as they walked to Emmaus. At the table, their eyes were opened and the resurrected Lord was revealed to them. The interpreted word enabled them to see what they were experiencing at the table. As they came to the table, they were still living in Friday, but at the table they experienced the meaning of the "first day of the week." Their

"Friday" had now become "Sunday." Their hopelessness had turned to joy; their mourning had turned into dancing.But wait, didn't the Teacher say earlier that the dead have it better than the living (4:1-2), and now he says just the opposite?

ACTS 20:7a, 11-12

7a *On the first day of the week, when we were gathered together to break bread, Paul talked with them...* 11 *And when Paul had gone up and had broken bread and eaten, he conversed with them a long while, until daybreak, and so departed.* 12 *And they took the youth away alive, and were not a little comforted.*

They Went Home Comforted

The newly baptized disciples in Act 2 devoted themselves to the breaking of the bread. They practiced it daily in Jerusalem. Perhaps part of the three thousand who gathered in the temple and homes of hospitable believers in Jerusalem were travelers from distant places like Rome or Mesopotamia. They would return home eventually but while in Jerusalem they depended upon the hospitality of their brothers and sisters. Daily meals became a way of sharing food and resources with these new believers.

As we read through the book of Acts, Luke does not provide many stories of believers gathered to break bread. He assumes that readers will recognize the devotion of the first disciples will continue as the kingdom spreads across the Roman empire. Disciples, then, will continue to listen to the teaching of the apostles and enjoy fellowship, including prayers, shared resources, and the breaking of bread.

After Acts 2, we do not see a group of disciples gathered to break bread until Acts 20:7-12 when Paul arrives in Troas, waits several days, and gathers with disciples in an upper room. Luke narrates the night in Troas with language that recalls or echoes Luke 24. In other words, Luke wants us to read Acts 20:7-12 in the light of Luke 24:13-35.

In both Luke 24 and Acts 20, disciples break bread together upon the first day of the week. In both contexts, there is a teaching of the word or exposition of Scripture. Both texts describe a resurrection from the dead where the dead one is presented as alive once again.

Common Language	Luke 24	Acts 20
Gathered Disciples	24:33	20:7
Breaking of Bread	24:30, 35	20:7, 11
Eating Together	24:42-43	20:11
First Day of the Week	24:1, 13	20:7
Teaching the Word (Greek: *logos*)	24:44	20:7
Conversation (Greek: *homileō*)	24:14-15	20:11
Resurrection	24:5, 46	20:10, 12
Fear	24:37-38	20:11
Living One (Greek: *zaō*)	24:5	20:12

Disciples in both episodes are gathered to break bread on the first day of the week in the presence of one raised from the dead.

The presence of Eutychus, the young man raised from the dead in Troas, is a concrete symbol of the meaning of the meal itself. They gathered to break bread, but they listened to Paul first. They did not break bread until Eutychus was raised from the dead. After retrieving Eutychus, the assembly went back upstairs and they broke bread. While the text says Paul broke bread and ate (a meal), this is a synecdoche for the whole. Paul did not eat alone. The assembly ate with Paul and the one who had been raised from the dead.

In the light of the echoes of Luke 24, the episode in Troas reminds us of the meaning of the breaking of the bread. It is eating in the presence of the resurrected Christ who is the actual host of the meal. In the context of Luke 24 and Acts 20, the meaning of the Lord's Supper or breaking of bread is the celebration of the resurrection which gives and promises life. We give thanks, rejoice in new life, and proclaim the gospel, the death and resurrection of Jesus the Messiah.

What is the experience of the disciples at Emmaus and Troas in relation to the Lord's Supper? What is the atmosphere or mood of their breaking of bread?

The conjunction of the first day of the week, resurrection, and breaking bread highlight the meaning of the meal. These three ideas converge to proclaim the resurrection of the Messiah who, as the Living One, hosts the table of the Lord to which his disciples are invited. While the Jerusalem church broke bread daily (probably due to the exigent circumstances of many guests in the city), the church at Troas apparently gathered weekly. The resurrection of Jesus, the first day of the week, and breaking bread are deeply intertwined so that the combination is a powerful testimony and experience of the gospel itself. If the breaking of bread is God's gift to celebrate the resurrection of Jesus, and the first day of the week is the symbol of that resurrection, then it makes a great deal of sense to celebrate the gospel every first day of week when we gather to proclaim the gospel.

Leaving that gathering where they broke bread together at the table of the resurrected one, the disciples took Eutychus "away alive, and were not a little comforted" (Acts 20:12). Though surrounded by suffering, chaos, and death in our own lives, we rise from the table comforted that death does not have the final say. We have just eaten with the living Messiah, and death has no ultimate power over us.

REVELATION 1:10, 17b-18

10 *I was in the Spirit on the Lord's day, and I heard behind me a voice like a trumpet...* 17b *saying, "Fear not, I am the first and the last,* 18 *and the living one. I died, and behold I am alive forevermore, and I have the keys of Death and Hades."*

Why Do We Eat on Sunday Like It is Still Friday?

While the Jerusalem church practiced a daily table, it appears the church ultimately adopted the habit of a weekly table. Acts 20:7 is apparently an example of this. This became the historic, but not exclusive, practice of the church throughout the centuries. The disciples of Jesus gathered every first day of the week to break bread or to celebrate the Eucharist (thanksgiving)—two ways of describing the same thing in the early church. For example, two early documents (ranging from AD 90-115) link together assembling, breaking bread, and the first day of the week. Didache 14:1 says, "On the Lord's day, after you have assembled together, break bread and give thanks." Ignatius wrote to the Ephesians (20:2), "assemble yourselves together... breaking bread, which is the medicine of immortality." Christians gathered weekly to eat the Lord's Supper on the first day of every week in both East and West (though not exclusively on the first day of the week) until the Reformation when Ulrich Zwingli (d. 1531) moved the Supper to a quarterly observance (once every three months).

A CLOSER LOOK: THE APOSTOLIC FATHERS

The collection of Christian writings known as the "Apostolic Fathers" is the earliest Christian works after the New Testament. Although most do not view these writings as on par with the Old and New Testaments, the Apostolic Fathers offer extraordinary insight into the life, thinking, and struggles of the generation of Christians after the New Testament. Most well known in this collection are the letters from Ignatius and Clement, as well as the Didache (Greek *didachē*, "instruction, teaching") of the Twelve Apostles.[13]

The early church interpreted the "Lord's day" as the first day of the week. On that day Jesus appeared to John in Revelation 1. Significantly, Jesus declares that he is the "living one" who holds "the

---

[13] For more, see the introduction in Michael William Holmes, ed., *The Apostolic Fathers: Greek Texts and English Translations* (Grand Rapids: Baker Books, 2007), 3-32.

keys of Death and Hades." He appears to John on the Lord's day as the resurrected Lord. To gather on the first day of the week to break bread as the assembly of the Lord is to proclaim the gospel, the death and resurrection of Jesus the Messiah.

As we saw in Luke 24 and Acts 20, there is a natural affinity between resurrection, the breaking of the bread, and the first day of the week. It is good and appropriate to eat with Jesus every week on his resurrection day, the day when new creation began. If the table was given to us as a way to reveal the resurrected Jesus, experience the presence of Jesus, and receive comfort and joy from God's victory over death, why would we omit this gift from our weekly assemblies? If God gave us this means to enjoy resurrection life and celebrate victory over death, why would we not celebrate it every first day of the week on the day of Jesus's own resurrection?

The central act of God in the Lord's Supper is the presence of the living host who assures us of the future. God is present at the table by the Spirit in the person of Christ the Lord. It is a celebration of life, victory, and hope. In fact, it is the experience of the future. At the table, we experience the future reality of the resurrection present in the person of the living host, Jesus. Certainly we remember his death just as we remember his whole life, but we do not remember him as one who remains in the grave or dying on the cross. We remember and celebrate his victory over death even as we also remember his loving sacrifice on the cross.

> **Does your experience of the Lord's supper tend to transform your "Fridays" into "Sundays"? Does it tend to move you from despair to hope? Why or why not?**

As we come to the table every week we are surrounded by all kinds of tragedies, wounds, and struggles. We all live with "Fridays" of one sort of another. We all know what it is like to grieve and sit by a grave like those who buried Jesus on that Friday so long ago. But Sunday is a day of hope. Breaking bread on the first day of the week transforms our Fridays into Sundays as we encounter the living Christ at the table. In the breaking of the bread, it is no longer Friday but Sunday. If we break bread on the first day of the week, why do we eat it like it is still Friday?

How might we adjust our practice of communion in the assembly to reflect more of the joy of the resurrection than a funeral at the tomb?

KEY IDEAS:

- The living, resurrected Messiah is made known in the breaking of the bread.
- The Lord's Supper proclaims hope and offers comfort in a world filled with death.
- The breaking of the bread is a Sunday (first day of the week) celebration rather than a mere Friday memory.

DISCIPLESHIP PROMPT:

Just as we followed Jesus into the water, so we follow Jesus to the table. We are invited to celebrate the Messiah's victory by sharing a meal with Jesus and with his disciples as part of the gathering of God's people. In this meal we are nourished by the living Christ who sustains us with his own eternal life. As we eat together, we are comforted and empowered. Rising from the table, we go home comforted but also commissioned to become bread for the world. We come to the table not for solace only but for strength to give ourselves for the world just as Christ gave himself for us. Reflect on these various types of nourishment that we receive the next time you gather around the table.

PRAYER:

God, "deliver us from the presumption of coming to this Table for solace only, and not for strength; for pardon only, and not for renewal." Through your gift of life at this Table, send us into the world to serve the world for your glory. May we become bread for the world, just as Christ became bread for us! In the name of Jesus, Amen.[14]

---

[14] This prayer is based on "Eucharistic Prayer C" from *The Book of Common Prayer.*

– 11 –

THEOLOGY OF BAPTISM—GOD WORKS THROUGH BAPTISM

Romans 6:1-11; Colossians 2:11-13; Galatians 3:26-29

> Through baptism we participate in the gospel and find our identity in Jesus, God's Messiah.

In the Acts of the Apostles, we learned that baptism was part of the conversion narrative of every disciple of Jesus. When people believed in the testimony about Jesus the Messiah, they were baptized and became part of the community of disciples dedicated to following Jesus. Paul was an early participant in that story. He was baptized by Ananias (Acts 9:18; 22:16). His apostolic church-planting mission baptized many others (Acts 16:5, 33; 18:8; 19:5), though he did not always do the baptizing himself (1 Cor 1:14-16).

When Paul writes to congregations of Christ-followers, he writes to baptized people. Nowhere in his letters does he tell people to get baptized. He does not attempt to persuade them because he assumes they already are baptized. Every use of the verb "baptize" in Paul's letters is in the past tense. For example, "For in one Spirit we were all baptized into one body" (1 Cor 12:13). Paul's letters are not evangelistic tracts seeking to persuade people to be baptized.

On the contrary, Paul's letters talk about baptism in order to deepen the recipient's understanding of the gospel and its implications for the people of God as disciples. Paul names baptism as a way of helping early disciples to fully understand the call on their lives and the meaning of their salvation. He remembers their baptism in order to deepen their discipleship, persuade them to embrace the forgiveness and life God has given in Christ, and to unite believers as people baptized into Christ and thus joined together in Christ.

ROMANS 6:3-4

3 Do you not know that all of us who have been baptized into Christ were baptized into his death? 4 We were buried therefore with him by baptism into death, in order that, just as Christ was raised from the dead by the glory of the Father, we too might walk in newness of life.

Baptized into Christ

We might say Paul's response was incredulous. He could not believe that disciples of Jesus might actually contend for such an opinion. "Do you not you know …" suggests Paul regards their baptism as fundamentally incompatible with the question's premise.

This was the question, "Are we to continue in sin that grace may abound?" (Rom 6:1). After all, one might argue, if there is more grace when there is more sin, why not continue to sin? Paul's response: your baptism provides the answer!

We cannot continue in sin, Paul wrote, because we have "died to sin." Yet, how did we die to sin? Disciples of Jesus should know the answer. "Do you not know that all of us who have been baptized into Christ Jesus were baptized into his death?" Through baptism we were united with the death of Christ, and the death of Christ put sin to death. Through baptism we died with Jesus, and if the death of Jesus was the death of sin, then we died to sin when we were buried with him. When we were buried with him through baptism, "our old self was crucified with" Jesus (Rom 6:6). Dying to sin not only means to be separated from sin (forgiveness) but also to take away its power (sanctification). To be dead to sin is to be "set free" from both the guilt and power of sin (Rom 6:7).

But baptism means more than death. It is also means resurrection life. If we are united with Christ's death, we are also united with his resurrection. We rise out of the watery grave of baptism to a new life. We arise empowered to "walk in newness of life." We are both "dead to sin," and "alive to God" (Rom 6:11). This life is not simply forgiveness but the capacity to subvert the powers of sin and its passions in our lives. Sin must no longer reign in our bodies. Rather, we are to present ourselves to God "as instruments for righteousness" (Rom 6:13). Neither the guilt nor the power of sin has "dominion" over us because we are grounded in the grace of God's gift of salvation rather than in the anxiety of working our way out from under sin's guilt and power (Rom 6:14). Thus, we are dead to sin (by the death of Jesus) and alive to God (by the resurrection of Jesus).

Baptism embodies this gracious reality. Baptism is a means by which God unites us to both the death and resurrection of Jesus. Through baptism we participate in the gospel, that is, the death and resurrection of Jesus. Baptism is a burial into the death of Christ where we die to sin by the death of Christ. We do not put ourselves to death, but the death of Jesus kills our sinful selves (the old person). By grace, we participate in the death which crucifies the body of sin. Also, by grace through baptism, we are resurrected with Christ so that the life we live is no longer our own; it is the life of Jesus. We do not raise ourselves to life, but the resurrection of Jesus gives our dead bodies life and empowers us to live a new life.

Baptism is a dynamic movement. We are united with Christ ("baptized into Christ"), united with his death ("baptized into his death"), and united with his resurrection ("buried with him by baptism" so that we too might be raised). Something happens in baptism. But it is not what we do; it is what God does. God unites us with Christ, and it is through God's power that we die to sin and are raised to life. This is God's doing, not ours.

How does baptism orient us to the nature of
salvation as past, present, and future?

How does baptism testify that we are saved, are
being saved, and will be saved (see Rom 5:10)?

Paul uses the language of means or instrumentality. He wrote, "We were buried therefore with him *by* baptism into death" (Rom 6:4). He uses the Greek preposition *dia* (by means of, through). This is one reason we can say baptism is a means of grace, that is, it is a means by which God works in our lives to effect our forgiveness (death to sin) and transformation (resurrection). Paul uses a similar expression in Titus 3:5: "[God] saved us, not because of works done by us in righteousness, but according to his own mercy, by [*dia*] the washing of regeneration and renewal of the Holy Spirit."

Romans 6:4 and Titus 3:5, of course, do not undermine the function of faith. We are saved through (*dia*) faith (Eph 2:8), and we will see in the next section that baptism is effective through (*dia*) faith (Col 2:12). Baptism as a means of grace does not function apart from faith. Rather, it participates in faith; baptism expresses faith. Consequently, baptism is a means of grace as it participates in the instrumentality of faith. To say baptism is a means of grace is not to say it is a work of salvation. On the contrary, it is to say that it participates in the function of faith itself. Baptism is a means of grace because God saves through faith, and faith is expressed in baptism.

COLOSSIANS 2:11-13

11 *In him also you were circumcised with a circumcision made without hands, by putting off the body of the flesh, by the circumcision of Christ,* 12 *having been buried with him in baptism, in which you were also raised with him through faith in the powerful working of God, who raised him from the dead.* 13 *And you, who were dead in your trespasses and the uncircumcision of your flesh, God made alive together with him, having forgiven us all our trespasses.*

Through Faith in the Power of God

Ephesians 2:8 says, "For by grace you have been saved through faith." Colossians 2:11-13 expands this brief statement. Paul told the Ephesians, "you were dead in the trespasses and sins" and "lived in the passions of our flesh," but "God made us alive together in Christ" (Eph 2:1, 3, 5). Here, in different but similar words, Paul tells the Colossians that they were once "dead in [their] trespasses and the uncircumcision of [their] flesh," but "God made [them] alive together with" Jesus (Col 2:13).

The "uncircumcision" of the Gentiles cut them off from the promises of God to Israel ("strangers to the covenants of promise," Eph 2:12), and their sins separated them from God ("dead"). They were without hope because they were disconnected from God's redemptive story in Israel. The Gentiles needed a path for inclusion in that story so they might become part of the story of Israel. They needed circumcision, which was the sign of God's covenant with Israel. It was a physical sign "in the flesh made by hands" (Eph 2:11). It signaled inclusion. It meant one was part of the people of God, the assembly of Israel.

In Christ, Gentiles receive a "circumcision made without hands." Clearly, this circumcision is not effected in the flesh but in the heart. This heart-circumcision is not new; it was part of what God effected in ancient Israel as well (Deut 10:16; 30:6; Jer 4:4). We may call it regeneration or renewal. To say something is not performed by human hands is, in effect, to say God does it through the Spirit. Ephesians for example, says our access to the Father is in Christ through the Spirit (2:11, 18), and God dwells in the new temple—the body of Christ—by the Spirit (2:22).

God circumcises the Gentiles by the Spirit in the "circumcision of Christ." Scholars debate whether this is a circumcision Christ performs on the Gentiles or whether it is the circumcision Christ underwent, that is, his death. If the "putting off the body of the flesh" is a reference to the death of Christ (which seems most probable), then the point is something like this: Jesus was circumcised when he was stripped of his flesh. The death of Christ effects spiritual circumcision.

In Christ, the Gentiles were circumcised because of the Messiah's death. The hearts of Gentiles are circumcised through the gospel.

But what does this have to do with baptism? If the Gentiles are circumcised in the death of Christ, how do they participate in that death? Colossians 2:12 answers the question: "having been buried with him in baptism." The participle ("having been buried") depends on the main verb in verse 11 ("you were circumcised"). In other words, they were circumcised by the death of Jesus when they were buried with him in baptism. Baptism, then, is a means (or at least an attendant circumstance) by which God works to circumcise hearts through a union with Christ in his death and resurrection. This is analogous to John 3:5 where Jesus says one must be "born of water and the Spirit." God circumcises the heart by the Spirit in the context of our burial with Christ in baptism.

Baptism, however, is not only a burial but a resurrection. Jesus was buried, but God raised him from the dead. We are buried with Jesus but raised with him as well. Though we were "dead" in our sins, God "made [us] alive together with him, having forgiven us all our trespasses" (Col 2:13). Through baptism we unite with the death of Christ as we are buried in water for the forgiveness of our sins, but we are also made alive in union with the resurrection of Christ because we have new life. We must be careful that we do not attribute the efficacy of baptism to our own obedience or the working of a plan. It is God who, by the Spirit, circumcises our hearts because of the circumcision (death) of Christ. This is God's work, not ours. As Paul says, we are "raised with [Jesus] through faith in the powerful working of God, who raised him from the dead" (Col 2:12). Only God can make anything come alive; only God raises the dead. We enter the water dead in our sins, and we come out of the water forgiven of our sins. This is God's doing. We are buried as dead people, and God causes us to live again. It is God's work.

At the same time, we submit to this burial as people dead in our sin, and we put our faith in what God is doing. We are raised to life "through faith" in God's working. Just as in Ephesians 2:8, we are saved by grace through faith, so here in Colossians 2:12, we are buried and raised in baptism through faith in God's work. Moreover, the effectual power of baptism is not what we believe about baptism but our trust in what God has done in the death and resurrection of Jesus. Our faith is in Jesus, not baptism.

Paul says all this to make a fundamental point: your salvation rests in the work of Christ. It is not based on ethnicity, circumcision, ascetic practices, or the keeping of festivals, sabbaths, and new moons. No human philosophy or sophistry will add anything to what God has done in Christ.

Our baptism testifies to the work of God in Christ by the Spirit. It reminds us that God's work is sufficient, and it is God who effects our salvation, including the forgiveness of sins. As baptized people, we were buried dead in our sins but raised free from sin and its debt.

GALATIANS 3:26-29

[26] *For in Christ Jesus you are all sons of God, through faith.* [27] *For as many of you as were baptized into Christ have put on Christ.* [28] *There is neither Jew nor Greek, there is neither slave nor free, there is no male and female, for you are all one in Christ Jesus.* [29] *And if you are Christ's, then you are Abraham's offspring, heirs according to the promise.*

Sons of God and Heirs of the Promise

We are all sons of God, even women! Perhaps it sounds strange to say that women as well as men are sons of God, but that is what Paul wrote. He did not say "children" of God; there is a word for that in

Greek. Rather, he explicitly said "sons (*huioi*) of God," which typically refers to males and excludes females. Men are sons, and women are daughters. But here we are "all sons of God." Why does Paul use this specific language?

Except under special circumstances, only sons inherited in both the Hebrew Bible and in Greco-Roman society. In fact, when there was no suitable male to inherit, Romans would often adopt male heirs to ensure a legacy. Women did not normally share in the inheritance of their fathers. Also, Gentiles were not heirs of God's promise to Abraham, and enslaved people did not inherit the estate of their masters when the masters died. When Paul says there is neither Jew nor Greek, neither enslaved nor free, and no male and female, he is talking about inheritance. No longer are there any ethnic, economic, or gender distinctions in relation to inheritance. We are all "sons" of God; we are all heirs.

God sent the Son, the Messiah, to be born of woman in order to redeem us "so that we might receive adoption as sons," and because we are "sons, God has sent the Spirit" of the Son "into our hearts, crying, 'Abba! Father!'" (Gal 4:4-6). God sends the Spirit into all of the sons of God, whether Jew or Gentile, enslaved or free, male or female. In Christ, we are all heirs to the promise of Abraham, free from enslavement "to the elementary principles of the world" (Ga 4:3), and there is no longer any male and female distinction in the distribution of the inheritance.

How does baptism fit into this picture? Paul announced that we are sons of God through faith "for as many of you as were baptized into Christ have put on Christ" (Gal 3:26-27). We become sons of God by being joined to or united with the Son of God, who is Christ Jesus. Further, we become heirs of the Abrahamic promise because we have been united to the heir, Jesus the Messiah. Since the promise belongs to the "offspring" of Abraham, and that "offspring" is the Messiah (Gal 3:16), everyone united to that seed or offspring is also an heir of the promise to Abraham.

Through our baptism into Christ, we "put on" Christ. In both Jewish and Greco-Roman culture, one's clothing identified their status, whether they were free or enslaved, male or female, or Jew or Gentile. It identified their economic and social standing in the culture. "Putting on Christ" is not so much a reference to putting on a new person in an ethical sense as in Eph 4:24 or Col 3:10 (though it may have those overtones). Rather, it alludes to a new identity or new status. The enslaved, Gentiles, and women are no longer outsiders but participants. They, too, share in this status—a son of God because they are united with the Son of God. They have been baptized into the Son of God.

> How does our baptismal identity transcend all other identities we have in the world? Why is this important for the church to embrace today?

Since we all share this new identity as sons of God, and we are all heirs of the promise to Abraham, we, therefore, are one in Christ. We have all been baptized into Christ and put on Christ, and consequently we are all one in Christ Jesus. No ethnic (Jew or Gentile), economic (free or enslaved), or gender (male and female) differentiations should impair our shared life as heirs of the promise. When any of these differences subvert our shared inheritance, our common sonship, and our shared status in the kingdom of God as sons of God, it overthrows the unity to which our baptism testifies.

KEY IDEAS:

- Through baptism we participate in the gospel as we are united with Christ.
- Baptism is a means by which God graciously acts for our salvation by forgiving our sins and animating our lives.
- Our baptism testifies to the identity God has given us through Christ in the Spirit.

DISCIPLESHIP PROMPT:

While we actively embrace following Jesus through submitting to baptism, God is the active agent who gives the grace that accompanies baptism. United with Christ and heirs of the promise, our baptism both graces us and forms us. We are graced through union with Christ in his death and resurrection, and we are formed as instruments of righteousness as we follow Jesus. We rise to walk a new life with circumcised hearts as part of a community that transcends all earthly boundaries. Just as we followed Jesus into the water and God met us there, so we follow Jesus into the world and God empowers us to become like Christ in every way. If you have not been baptized, will you prayerfully consider doing so? If you have been baptized, reflect on your spiritual growth since your baptism. What joys has God brought you since then? What did you struggle with then and do you struggle with it now?

PRAYER:

God, thank you for the grace you have given us through baptism. May we remember the vows we took at baptism and embrace the new life to which you called us in our baptism. Fill us with your Spirit daily so we might honor our baptisms as gifts of your grace. In name of Jesus, Amen.

– 12 –

THEOLOGY OF ASSEMBLY—ENJOYING
GOD AND ENCOURAGING EACH OTHER

Hebrews 10:19-25; 12:18-24; Mark 12:29-31

> Our assemblies, where God loves on us, we love on God, and we love on each other, participate in the heavenly assembly gathered around God's throne.

What we have traditionally called "the Epistle to the Hebrews" is actually a sermon. The author calls it "my word of exhortation" (Hebrews 13:22). Though this is the language of first century Judaism, today we call them sermons. "After the reading of the Law and the Prophets," the rulers of the synagogue invited Paul to address the assembly. "If you have any word of exhortation for the people," they asked, "say it." Then Paul, standing up, delivered what we would call a sermon (Acts 13:16-41).[15]

Hebrews does not begin like a letter, though it ends like it in its final verses. It begins like a teaching document, like a sermon. It reads like a speech: "time would fail me" (11:32), "of these things we cannot now speak in detail" (9:5), or "though we speak in this way (6:9). It is also filled with exhortations based on biblical texts, primarily the Psalms. Its style is like a Jewish-Greek homily, including the use of rhetorical questions and a catalog of witnesses from the Hebrew Scriptures.

---

[15] For more on Hebrews as a sermon, see Ben Witherington, *Letters and Homilies for Jewish Christians: A Socio-Rhetorical Commentary on Hebrews, James and Jude* (Downers Grove, IL: IVP Academic, 2007), 20-22.

We might legitimately imagine, then, the preacher in Hebrews addressing a congregation. Perhaps this is a written version of a sermon shared with the congregation so it might serve a wider audience. Today we provide web links to sermons recently delivered in assemblies. Hebrews, in essence, is what this preacher said to an assembled church.

The sermon addresses a discouraged group of people. While once they flourished and faithfully suffered persecution in their beginning, now the congregation is fatigued and stressed. A new persecution is on the horizon, and they have lost the zeal of their former years. They are drifting as if they are slowly dying, and some have already abandoned the faith. This "word of exhortation" invites the congregation to remember what God has done in Jesus, to renew their faith in God's provision, and to return to their former boldness. The preacher addresses the assembly of God to call them to perseverance and faithfulness in the face of the coming persecution and discouraging losses in the congregation.

Perhaps it is a message we need to hear as well.

HEBREWS 10:19-25

19 *Therefore, brothers, since we have confidence to enter the holy places by the blood of Jesus,* 20 *by the new and living way that he opened for us through the curtain, that is through his flesh,* 21 *and since we have a great high priest over the house of God,* 22 *let us draw near with a true heart in full assurance of faith, with our hearts sprinkled clean from an evil conscience and our bodies washed with pure water.* 23 *Let us hold fast the confession of our hope without wavering, for he who promised is faithful.* 24 *And let us consider how to stir up one another to love and good works,* 25 *not neglecting to meet together, as is the habit of some, but encouraging one another, and all the more as you see the Day drawing near.*

Continue to Assemble

The highpoint of this "word of exhortation" is Heb 10:19-25. The preacher has argued that Jesus is better than the angels, better than Moses, better than the Levitical priests, better than Israel's high priest, and better than the Mosaic covenant. The person and work of Jesus the

Messiah fulfills the hopes of Israel and provides a "new and living way" into the presence of God.

We enter the Holy of Holies through the gospel based on the priestly work of Jesus the Messiah. On the analogy of the Jerusalem temple, we enter the presence of God through the curtain of the sacrificial death of Jesus and his intercessory presence in the Holy of Holies. We have direct access into God's most holy place, into the sanctuary of God's presence. This is why some name the spaces where believers gather "sanctuaries." That space is not holy in and of itself, but it becomes holy when the church gathers to enter the Holy of Holies as an assembled people. "We have the confidence to enter" the holies because of what God did in Jesus by the Spirit. Our new high priest leads us into the most holy place where he continues to intercede for us as high priest!

> How would understanding the "throne room" context of our assemblies change our attitudes toward the assembly? What attitudes should we have given our entrance into the Holy of Holies?

The scripture quoted above is actually one long sentence in Greek. Because of what Jesus has done, the preacher invites us to pursue assembling together in order to encourage each other. At the same time, the preacher identifies the function and purpose of the assembly itself. The bare bones of verses 19-25 runs something like this (with spacing to depict the flow of thought):

Since we have access to the heavenly sanctuary (19-21),
    let us draw near to God (22),
    let us hold fast our profession of hope (23),
    let us stir each other up (24)
        not neglecting the assembly but encouraging each other (25).

Rather than neglecting the assembly, we gather in order to encourage each other. But there is more happening than mutual

139

encouragement, as important as that is. The preacher's exhortations characterize the assembly as a place of communion with God, profession of faith, and mutual inspiration.

First, we draw near to God. This Hebraic expression means to go before the divine presence where we encounter God. We draw near to God just as Israel did (see Heb 10:1). Like Israel, we draw near with an existing relationship through faith, having our hearts sprinkled by the blood of Jesus (Exod 29:1) and our bodies washed in water (Exod 29:4). Because of the work of Jesus we boldly enter God's holy dwelling place.

Second, we profess our faith. Through assembly we hold fast to our confession of hope. We assemble in hope based upon God's own faithfulness. We publicly confess our faith in what God has done and is doing. We persevere in faith because we know God is faithful. Assembly, then, is a place where together we proclaim our faith and hope. When we assemble, we commit to continue in that faith and hope despite the discouragement and hostility that surrounds us in the world.

Third, we stir each other up. Through assembly we stir each other up to love and good works. When we assemble, we pay attention to or "consider" each other, not for negative ends but for positive ones. The preacher calls us to the sort of assembly that revels in the love we have for each other and produces a community filled with good works. In other words, the assembly ought to send us into the world to serve each other and the world. We assemble to love on each other and build a community devoted to good works.

I think the first point is foundational to the other two. Assembly is where disciples of Jesus encounter God. As an assembled people, we participate in the mission of God and are sent from the presence of God to minister in the kingdom. God is an active participant in the assembly who transforms us and communes with us. The assembly is an assembly of God *with* the people and not simply an assembly *of* the people.

That is why we "go to church"!

HEBREWS 12:18-24

[18] *For you have not come to what may be touched, a blazing fire and darkness and gloom and a tempest* [19] *and the sound of a trumpet and a voice whose words made the hearers beg that no further messages be spoken to them.* [20] *For they could not endure the order that was given, "If even a beast touches the mountain, it shall be stoned."* [21] *Indeed, so terrifying was the sight that Moses said, "I tremble with fear."* [22] *But you have come to Mount Zion and to the city of the living God, the heavenly Jerusalem, and to innumerable angels in festal gathering,* [23] *and to the assembly of the firstborn who are enrolled in heaven, and to God, the judge of all, and to the spirits of the righteous made perfect,* [24] *and to Jesus, the mediator of a new covenant, and to the sprinkled blood that speaks a better word than the blood of Abel.*

Going to Church

Unfortunately, some have reduced "going to church" to the only sacred moment in their lives. It is as if we "go to church" on Sunday, and then the rest of the week belongs to us. This fails to recognize that we are always already the church everywhere we go. We are the body of Christ whether assembled together, working our jobs, caring for our children, or taking classes at school.

Nevertheless, there is a sense in which we do "go to church." The preacher of Hebrews encourages us to assemble. In fact, the preacher wants us to assemble as much as possible, whether on Sunday or other days, whether small or large, whether the whole congregation or in small groups, whether in the building or in the park. What makes an assembly is the intention to draw near to God in faith, hope, and love. When we go to church, that is, when we assemble with other disciples of Jesus, we enter the presence of God together. We draw near to God in God's heavenly space as a community.

The preacher contrasts Israel's experience of God's presence at Sinai (Exod 19:12-13; Deut 9:19) and the experience of God's presence among assembled disciples of Jesus in the present. Sinai was a terrifying, holy, and awe-inspiring experience for Israel. It was their "day of assembly" (Deut 10:4; 18:16). The presence of God was revealed on the mountain through thundering, shakings, and lightning. It was a holy mountain because God's holy presence was there. That holiness, however, distanced people from God. They had limited access to the mountain. They could not even touch it.

> **In what ways does the assembly transcend the limits of space and time? How does the assembly unite us with the past, present, and future?**

However, with a new high priest, disciples of Jesus draw near to a different mountain. While Israel drew near to Mount Sinai, we draw near to Mount Zion. The verb "come" (Heb 12:18, 22) is the same word that appears in 10:22 ("draw near"). It is a worship term; it is about entrance into God's presence (Heb 4:16; 7:25; 10:1, 22; 11:6). Israel encountered God in a terrifying but awe-inspiring way at Sinai, but now the church comes to God with both joy and reverential awe as we experience the hope of God's future for us. As an assembly, we enter God's presence with boldness and delight. We come to where God lives (Mt. Zion or heavenly Jerusalem). The preacher described this divine dwelling-place not only by its surroundings and location but by who is gathered there (in addition to God and Jesus).

Innumerable angels in festal gathering. Angels surround the throne of God and live in the holy city. They worship God and celebrate the redemption God has accomplished through Jesus. They sing, "Worthy is the Lamb" as well as "Holy, Holy, Holy." The angelic chorus surrounds us in our assemblies. In fact, we join our voices to the angelic choir when we sing in our assemblies.

To the assembly of the firstborn who are enrolled in heaven. This is the company of the redeemed. They have their names written in the book of life. It is the church universal that still lives upon the earth. Literally, it reads: "assembly of the firstborn ones." When we assemble, we go to this church (assembly). We join the saints from all over the world who are gathered around God's throne. Whether one is in Singapore or New York, Mexico City or Berlin, all God's people are assembled in the same space—the heavenly Jerusalem.

To the spirits of the righteous made perfect. The "spirits of righteous persons" was a well-known idiom for dead saints in Jewish intertestamental literature (see Jub 23:30-31; 1 En 22:9; 102:4; 103:3-4). These are the witnesses who faithfully persevered and have claimed the victory of faith (Heb 11:4, 7). They are "perfected" in their heavenly glory. The righteous dead are, in some sense, gathered around the throne, and when we draw near to God, we enter the same holy space where they continue to live and worship God. In other words, I go to church to share the same space with others who have died in the Lord, including those whom we love dearly but miss so badly in the present.

> **What comfort do you derive from the realization that when we gather as an assembly that we also gather with those who have already died?**
>
> **As we gather today, what does that mean for our communion, fellowship, and worship?**
>
> **How does that revision or reimagine the assembly for you?**

When disciples of Jesus gather, they assemble in the throne room of God as a community and receive a foretaste of the future. The preacher tells us that disciples on earth participate in that reality. We come (approach, draw near) and join the assembly of God's creation in the throne room. We come to God by the blood of Jesus, and we experience the fellowship of angels, the church throughout the world, and all the departed saints.

MARK 12:29-31

²⁹ *Jesus answered, "The most important is, 'Hear, O Israel: The Lord our God, the Lord is one.* ³⁰ *And you shall love the Lord your God with all your heart and with all your soul and with all your mind and with all your*

strength.' [31] *The second is this: 'You shall love your neighbor as yourself.' There is no other commandment greater than these.*"

When We Assemble: A Dynamic of Love

The scribe responded to Jesus by noting that these two commandments—love of God and love of neighbor—are more important than "all whole burnt offerings and sacrifices." Or, Jesus put it this way, "on these two commandments depend all the Law and the Prophets" (Matt 22:40). Our life with God is grounded in love and expressed in love. Given that is true, we might also say that our assemblies are saturated with love, or at least God intends them to be.

> **In what ways do we love on God in the assembly, and in what ways does God love on us? And how do we love on each other?**

When we assemble, we love on each other. Assembly provides an opportunity for mutual encouragement, comfort, and edification. It is a moment of shared life through songs, prayers, teaching, and table. Love must characterize our assemblies or else it is like a "noisy gong" (1 Cor 13:1-3). Unfortunately, in Corinth, the assembly is where the poor were humiliated (1 Cor 11:22) and egotistical self-promoters competed with others by promoting their gifts (1 Cor 14). Their Supper did not lovingly share with those who had little. Rather, the poor had to fend for themselves. They used gifts to distinguish the superior from the inferior rather than using them for the common good. Their prayers and praises did not prioritize encouraging and comforting others but promoted their own gifts as tokens of their approval from God.

What kind of love should shape our assemblies? The sort described in 1 Cor 13. Love is diminished when actors perform rather than encourage. Love is diminished when assemblies cater to an attractional consumerism rather than confronting us with the reality of God's holy presence. Love is diminished when traditional preferences become immutable rules rather than exploring and utilizing the full range of gifts God has given the church. Love is never easy, and loving each other within the assembly is not easy either. Miscommunication, inadvertent comments, unannounced changes, liturgical arrangements, seating changes, changes in the practice of the table, etc. become occasions for offense, misunderstanding, and hurt feelings. But love, authentic love, covers a multitude of offenses. When we assemble, let us love one another.

When we assemble, we love on God. Psalm 116 is the grateful praise of one who had been delivered from death, and the psalmist responded to God in the presence of all the people. In the assembly, the psalmist declares, "I love the Lord!" When Israel gathered, they loved God through praise and thanksgiving, and on many occasions, through lament as well.

The Gospel of Luke describes a woman who was burdened by a deep conviction of sin but moved by a love for the one who forgave her. The "sinner" brought a gift to Jesus, fell at his feet, and loved him by tenderly kissing and anointing his feet. This is a narrative picture of worship where kneeling and kissing are the root actions that express this kind of worshipful prostration (*proskuneō*). Her act, in the words of Jesus, are acts of love. She loved Jesus.

Loving God as a community in the assembly is part of prostrating ourselves before God and kissing the face of God. We humbly fall on our face before God as we acknowledge God's greatness, holiness, and glory. We praise, honor, and fear God. It is also an act of intimacy, a kind of "kiss" whereby we express our love for God. We adore, cherish, and treasure God. We experience God's presence among us and participate in the dynamic and unending love of the Father, Son, and Spirit. When we assemble, we delight in that loving relationship and participate in it.

When we assemble, God loves on us. Too often God is regarded as inactive in our assemblies as if God passively sits on the throne to receive our praise as a mere spectator. This can even degenerate into an egotistical conception of God who says something like, "I am God, give me praise, this is why I created you and if you don't worship me, I'll zap you." It can reduce God to an Ego that needs stroking and approval.

When we love God, it is only because God has first loved us. That love is the ground of our response to God. When we assemble, God is already loving on us, and God continues to love us in and through the assembly. God is an active participant in the assembly rather than a mere spectator. But what does it mean to say God loves on us in the assembly?

God delights in us and rejoices over us (Zeph 3:17). God rests among us as God dwells among us, and this rest is the taste of sweet fellowship. God honors, blesses, and glorifies us (Zeph 3:20). As we enter the assembly, in part because we enter it with Jesus, we hear the words, "Blessed is [the one] who comes in the name of the Lord" (Psa 118:26). God's presence transforms and sanctifies us. Assembling is part of our spiritual formation where God works in and through us. God forgives and renews when we assemble together. And God graciously lifts us up into the heavenly throne room where we gather with all God's angels and saints (both living and dead) to enjoy God's presence.

When we assemble, we love God, we love each other, and God loves us. Who wouldn't want to be part of that?

KEY IDEAS:

- Assembling is an act of faith where we draw near to God, stir each other up to good works, and publicly confess our faith and hope.
- Our assemblies enter the throne room of God where we encounter God's loving presence as a community.
- We experience assembly as a relational and mutual lovefest: God loves on us, we love on God, and we love on each other.

DISCIPLESHIP PROMPT:

Disciples of Jesus assemble. They assemble to encourage one another and to draw near to God together. When we enter that space, we are reoriented to the glory of the risen Christ and the sovereignty of God. We encounter God for the sake of renewal, and we encourage each other for the sake of the mission. We enter into the throne room of

God to praise God, and we are sent from God's presence to serve the world. We follow Jesus as we ascend into the heavenlies to draw near to God, and we follow Jesus into the world as we are sent on mission from the heavenlies into the world. When you assemble with your brothers and sisters in Christ, look for one or two people or a family whom you can love on in a meaningful way.

PRAYER:

God, as we draw near to you in Jesus through your Holy Spirit, we bow down before you and praise you for your wondrous grace. We ask you to stir our hearts with your love and fill us with your Spirit that we might encourage each other. Send us, dear Father, into the world to love it just as you loved the world by sending your Son into it. May our lives bear witness to the power of your love. In the name of Jesus, Amen.

– 13 –

THEOLOGY OF THE LORD'S SUPPER—
COMMUNING WITH GOD AND EACH OTHER

1 Corinthians 10:14-17; 11:17-34

At the Lord's Supper, we commune with God and each other as we embody the gospel in our communal practices.

Throughout their history, Israel observed meals where they ate their sacrifices. They also conducted weekly Shabbat meals every Sabbath. These were significant and constant expressions of faith and community in Israel. When they ate the sacrifices, they ate with God, renewed their covenant with God, and enjoyed God's communion at the table. They celebrated God's life among them with meals consisting of sacrificed meat, bread, and drink. This was the heritage of early Jewish disciples of Jesus.

Religious meals were also pervasive in the Greco-Roman world. The temples sacrificed the animals, and worshippers ate the sacrifices at communal meals. Those meals were sometimes hosted in a banquet room at the temple and, at other times, in private homes where the host welcomed guests. Often these meals were connected to some kind of association attached to a particular trade guild (like leather-workers) or club (like a fireman's association). Greco-Roman cities, like Corinth, were saturated in the practice of religious meals. This was the heritage of early Gentile disciples of Jesus.

It is no surprise, then, that early disciples of Jesus gathered for a meal to eat the sacrifice (body and blood of Jesus) just as Israel and Greco-Roman religionists did. For many today the idea of "religious meal" appears rather odd. Many Christians do not participate in any such meals, and the Lord's Supper is no longer a full meal or supper for most practicing believers. The meal is symbolized in the bread and cup. While there is nothing wrong with such symbolism, it does not fully represent the sort of experience early followers of Jesus had. Like their Jewish ancestors, and similar to their Greco-Roman religious neighbors, the early disciples of Jesus ate meals together. They called it "the table of the Lord" (1 Cor 10:21) or "the Lord's Supper" (1 Cor 11:20).

1 CORINTHIANS 10:16-17

16 *The cup of blessing that we bless, is it not a participation in the blood of Christ? The bread that we break, is it not a participation in the body of Christ.* 17 *Because there is one bread, we who are many are one body, for we all partake of the one bread.*

Communion

When disciples of Jesus assembled around a table to eat the bread and drink the fruit of the vine, they proclaimed the gospel of Jesus. They continued the table practices of Israel, and those practices found their fulfillment in the broken bread and the cup of thanksgiving at the table of Jesus. In fact, Paul encouraged them to embrace the continuity between the tables in Israel and the table of the Lord. "Consider the people of Israel," he wrote (1 Cor 10:18).

In contrast, the tables of the Greco-Roman sacrifices were offered to idols, not the God of Israel. Consequently, Paul begins this section in 1 Cor with the imperative: "flee from idolatry" (10:14). "You cannot," Paul wrote, "drink the cup of the Lord and the cup of demons. You cannot partake of the table of the Lord and the table of demons." To do so is to "provoke the Lord to jealousy" (10:21-22). When disciples of Jesus sit at the table of demons and eat sacrifices offered to idols, they become "participants with demons" (10:20). In other words, those who sit at the table of demons affirm the life of those demons and fellowship them.

Israel, of course, succumbed to that danger. They turned from the living God to the golden calf at Mount Sinai. At the same mountain where Israel gathered to hear the word of God and the leaders of Israel ate with God on the mountain, the people turned to idolatry and indulged in sexual immorality at the foot of the holy mountain (1 Cor 10:7-8). The temptation was the same for early disciples, especially since many came from an idolatrous background and the culture promoted those table practices for economic (trade unions conducted business at them), social (expressions of status and peer pressure), and religious (worship of the gods, even the emperor) reasons. The question is, will disciples in Corinth provoke the Lord to jealousy?

Why does eating and drinking at the table of the Lord exclude participation in the table of demons and idolatrous relationships? This raises a question about the meaning of the table. Its fundamental meaning is communion, fellowship, or participation. Each of those words are potential translations of the Greek word *koinōnia*. When we break the bread and eat it, it is a *koinōnia* in the body of Christ. When we drink the cup, it is a *koinōnia* in the blood of Christ.

What exactly does that mean? Perhaps at its root, it affirms a commonality or a common-union. It is a shared reality. When we eat the bread, we participate in the body of Christ, and when we drink the cup, we participate in the blood of Christ. This affirms, at the very least, a spiritual reality that disciples share with the exalted Christ, and we share it together as a community. Since we all "partake" of the same bread and cup, which are the body and blood of Christ, we are united as one body in Christ. To partake is to experience that spiritual reality. We commune with God in Christ through the bread and cup. To eat and drink is to share in the body and blood of Christ; it is an experience of the gospel. It means we share in the benefits of the altar. We commune with God; we sit at table with God in peace and fellowship.

What is God doing at the table? There is an active mutuality here—God communes with us through the blood and body of Christ and we commune with God through the bread and cup. God is not a spectator at the table. God communes with those who eat and drink, and God unites us through the Spirit with everyone partaking of the body and blood. This communion transcends space and time as we commune with all saints around the globe and throughout history while, at the same time, it is a communion in the present with those who sit at the table around us. God in Christ initiates the communion of this table, extends it, and effects it. We commune with each other because God has first initiated communion with us.

The table, then, visibly constitutes the unity of the church. When we share the one loaf, the many become one because the bread is one—it is the body of Christ. When the assembly eats from the same table, they give concrete witness to the oneness of the body. There is one loaf and there is one body though we are many members. The one bread visibly expresses that the many members are one body.

How does the Lord's Supper express unity and community within the church? How does the form in which we observe the supper either enhance or diminish that unity and community?

This is why we must flee idolatry. United with Christ at the table, we cannot sit at the table of demons. United with Christ at the table, we are a community of people distinct from other communities. We cannot serve two masters.

Consequently, when we sit at the table of the Lord, we cannot also sit at the tables of greed, sexual exploitation, injustice, or any other idols of modern culture. We cannot sit at the table of the Lord and then comfortably and self-righteously sit at the table of greed and gossip on another day. Our commitment to the gospel at the table of the Lord transcends all other allegiances and rejects everything hostile to the gospel.

---

1 CORINTHIANS 11:20-22

20 *When you come together, it is not the Lord's supper that you eat.* 21 *For in eating, each one goes ahead with his own meal. One goes hungry, another gets drunk.* 22 *What! Do you not have houses to eat and drink in? Or do you despise the church of God and humiliate those who have nothing? What shall we say to you? Shall I commend you in this? No, I will not.*

The Gospel Table

What was happening in Corinth that would generate such a direct rebuke? The presence of "divisions" (11:18) and "factions" (11:19) disrupted the supper of the Lord. Whatever else this involved, the result was that the poor were humiliated by Corinth's practice. It boggles the mind that in the assembly of the Lord there would be a division between the rich and poor at the table of the Lord. But it seems that though the church was gathered to eat the Lord's Supper, they ate their own supper in such a way that the poor went hungry. The rich, who had their own homes to eat in and had plenty of food to satisfy the poor, did not wait for the arrival of those who had nothing in order to share a meal together. The poor not only went hungry, but they were humiliated and despised by how their brothers and sisters treated them. Paul would rather the rich eat something at home before they come to the assembly if they are so hungry that they can't wait for the poor to arrive.

The assembly in Corinth gathered for a supper (*deipnon*; 11:20, 21, 25). This was the regular evening meal in the Greco-Roman world. It usually came in two parts: the banquet meal followed by conversation around the table (typically known as a *symposium*), which often included some form of worship to the gods. The Corinthian assembly seems to

153

have followed this practice as they gathered for a meal (described in 11:17-34) and then remained for conversation, mutual encouragement, and the praise of God (much like 1 Cor 14).

The Corinthian believers, it seems, came together to eat a meal (11:20-22, 27-28, 33) as a church (assembly, 11:18), and then enjoyed a time of mutual edification and worship as a church (assembly, 14:23). The problem was that Greco-Roman banquets were often occasions of social stratification, drunkenness, and disorderliness. Apparently, this social habit bled over into Corinth's assemblies. Moreover, the way these Corinthian believers practiced the meal cohered with Greco-Roman expectations of social segregation. Rather than subverting such practices with a communion worthy of gospel hospitality, they maintained social and economic divisions between the rich and the poor.

What is the problem in Corinth? Why is there such dysfunction in the assembly surrounding the Lord's Supper in Corinth?

Paul cites the tradition of the Last Supper in order to underscore the seriousness of this breach. This is not to turn the supper into a somber affair, but recognizes that the supper is rooted in the gospel. Grounded in the gospel of the death and resurrection of Jesus, the table must reflect the table values of the kingdom of God. There can be no division between the rich and poor, between Jew and Gentile, or between male and female. This is a gospel table, not the table of the rich, Jews, or men.

It is the place where we proclaim the gospel! When we eat and drink, Paul wrote, we "proclaim the Lord's death until he comes" (1 Cor 11:26). The death of Christ is good news rather than sad news. In fact, Paul probably uses "death" here as a synecdoche for "death and resurrection," just as he earlier said that he preached nothing but Christ crucified (1 Cor 2:2). Paul did not exclude resurrection in his preaching. The same is true here: to proclaim the death of Christ is to proclaim the gospel, which includes the story of Jesus and especially

154

his resurrection as well as his death. We boast and rejoice in the death of Christ. The gospel is good news.

The "Lord's Supper" is the norm. It is his table, not ours, which he inaugurated through his death and resurrection. Therefore, we ought to treat each other as fellow servants, as fellow-members of the body. Just as the gospel is for all, so the supper is for all who share faith in the gospel. The meal ought to proclaim the gospel, but wealthy Corinthian Christians were undermining the gospel itself. They did not reflect the values of Christ. The seriousness of the table is clear from the warnings of judgment for those who fail to eat and drink in a worthy manner (more on that in a moment).

Some read this section as if Paul does not want anyone to eat a meal at the table of the Lord. But Paul counsels them to continue to eat the supper though they should wait for everyone (or, welcome everyone) so that no one will go hungry. In the context of this communal meal, where food is shared in communion with God and each other, Paul specifies three instructions for Corinth.

- **Instruction 1:** wait until (or welcome) everyone arrives before you eat the supper.
- **Instruction 2:** if you are hungry, eat something at home before you assemble so you can wait for everyone to arrive.
- **Instruction 3:** Paul will settle everything else when he arrives.

Paul does not say, "don't eat" but "wait" (or, welcome). This is the Lord's Supper, so the community waits for the arrival of the whole church and welcomes both rich and poor, enslaved and free, male and female. Perhaps some tarried because they were slaves who served at the timing of their masters. Whatever the reason, Paul wants the community to share their food with each other at one table rather than a divided table or a table that excludes some due to timing or economic status. At the table of the Lord, the rich ought to welcome the poor, and if they do not, then it is not the Lord's Supper that they eat but their own.

How can we enhance the horizontal or communal dimension of the supper in our assemblies?

155

1 CORINTHIANS 11:27

27 Whoever, therefore, eats the bread and drinks the cup of the Lord in an unworthy manner will be guilty concerning the body and blood of the Lord.

Eating Worthy of the Gospel

Paul expects disciples of Jesus to eat the Lord's Supper in a worthy manner. Unfortunately, many today have misunderstood this to mean that we must be worthy to eat or must have lived exemplary lives the previous week without any major or mortal sins. However, when we feel unworthy or despair over our "worthlessness," this is the moment we should run to the table to receive grace and mercy. The table offers grace to those who seek the Lord at the table. When burdened with guilt and grief, we don't run away from the table. Rather, we run to it. The point, however, is not about the status and dignity of the participants but the manner in which they participate. In other words, it is not about private introspection or whether we are concentrating on the right thing and attitude, but how we participate as a community. It is not about whether we are focused on the cross and thinking about it with sadness and perhaps even shame, but whether we are sharing the table in a cruciform way, in a way that honors Jesus. Do we eat and drink in a way that professes the gospel rather than subverting it?

That one must not eat or drink in an "unworthy manner" refers to the divisive context in which it was being eaten at Corinth (11:27). Christians must "discern the body" when eating (11:29). Does this mean the body of Christ in the bread? I don't think so since it is likely Paul would have said "body and blood" (as he did in 11:27) if this were his meaning. Rather, it addresses the problem at Corinth, which is the unity of the church (Christ's body). Paul had earlier made the same shift from "body" where "body" refers to the flesh of Christ, to "body" where "body refers to the church in 1 Cor 10:16-17. He does the same thing here. The communal body of Christ must examine itself about the manner in which it conducts the supper. If we eat and drink in a way that dishonors Christ or subverts the gospel, then many will become weak and ill as they fall under God's judgment for defaming the table of the Lord (11:30).

156

What does it mean to eat the Lord's Supper in an unworthy manner? What does it mean to "discern" the body of Christ in eating the Lord's Supper? How does this shape our practice today?

At the same time, we must sit at the table in a worthy manner; we must eat and drink *worthily*. To answer what that means, let us stay within the context of Paul's letter to the Corinthians. In that light, I suggest the following three points. They are not exhaustive, of course, but suggestive.

We sit at the table of the Lord worthily when we embody the gospel at the table. The Corinthians failed to embody the gospel because they did not invite the poor to the same table as the rich. Whereas Jesus invited all to his table, rich and poor, the Corinthians practiced a social stratification that excluded the poor. This, in effect, denied the gospel. Since the gospel is for all, the table is for all. To exclude the poor from the table is to deny one of the key elements of the mission of the gospel: to preach the good news to the poor.

We sit at the table of the Lord worthily when we embody the unity of the body of Christ at the table. Rather than united around the table, the Corinthians used the table as a place to promote its divisions. Whether that division was economic (rich and poor) or sectarian ("I am of Peter" vs. "I am of Apollos"), the result is the same: the body of Christ is torn apart. At the very moment when God is spiritually uniting the one body through the one bread, we subvert that unity by eating in a way that divides the body rather than uniting it. One way we eat unworthily is when we eat as divided people, and such division subverts the gospel itself.

We sit at the table of the Lord worthily when we profess our allegiance to Christ at the table. The Corinthians were eating at two tables—the table of the Lord and the table of demons. In doing so, they ate unworthily. At the table of the Lord, we renew our covenant with God and recommit ourselves to the path of discipleship. Consequently, if we eat with a dual commitment rather than a singular

157

allegiance, we do not live "worthy of the gospel" (Phil 1:27). To come to the table with a divided allegiance is to eat in an unworthy manner.

KEY IDEAS:

- Communion is the primary meaning of the Lord's Supper.
- Communion is both vertical (with God) and horizontal (with each other).
- Through this communion God forms the many members into one body as they participate in the gospel of Jesus the Messiah.

DISCIPLESHIP PROMPT:

The table of the Lord is a renewal of our covenant with God whereby we recommit to following Jesus. It is also a means by which we commune with God and each other in the gospel. God invites us to enjoy the fellowship of the Triune God, calls us to imitate the life of Jesus, and to accept each other for the sake of the gospel. At the table we proclaim the gospel of Jesus in word and deed. The next time you partake of the Lord's Supper, reflect on how you are proclaiming the gospel of Christ, and that following Jesus is the central task of your life.

PRAYER:

God, we yearn to commune with you. Thank you for the gift of the bread and the fruit of the vine—the body and blood. Make us one with you and with each other. We ask, O Father, that you use this table to form us into the image of your Son, as the body of Christ, through your Spirit. In the Name of Jesus, Amen.

BIBLIOGRAPHY

Campbell, Alexander. *Christian Baptism with its Antecedents and Consequents.* Bethany: Campbell, 1851.

———. "Dialogue on Heresy." *Millennial Harbinger* 3 (August 1832): 403-6.

———. "Regeneration." *Millennial Harbinger Extra* 4 (August 1833): 337-84.

Campbell, Thomas. "An Address to All our Christian Brethren, Upon the Necessity and Importance of the Actual Enjoyment of our Holy Religion." *Millennial Harbinger* Third Series 1, no. 5 (May 1844): 199-203.

Hicks, John Mark. *Around the Bible in 80 Days: The Story of God from Creation to New Creation.* Abilene, TX: Abilene Christian University Press, 2022.

———. *Enter the Water, Come to the Table: Baptism and the Lord's Supper in Scripture's Story of New Creation.* Abilene, TX: Abilene Christian University Press, 2014.

Hicks, John Mark, Johnny Melton, and Bobby Valentine. *A Gathered People: Revisioning the Assembly as Transforming Encounter.* Abilene, TX: Leafwood Publishers, 2007.

Holmes, Michael William, ed. *The Apostolic Fathers: Greek Texts and English Translations.* Grand Rapids: Baker Books, 2007.

Lockyer, Sr., Herbert, ed. "Midrash." In *Nelson's Illustrated Bible Dictionary.* Nashville: Thomas Nelson, 1986.

Moo, Douglas. *The Epistle to the Romans.* NICNT. Grand Rapids: Eerdmans, 1996.

Morgan, Carey. "The Place of the Lord's Supper in the Movement." In *Centennial Convention Report*, edited by W. R. Warren, 464-78. Cincinnati: Standard, 1910.

Richardson, Robert. *Memoirs of Alexander Campbell*. Philadelphia: J. B. Lippincott & Co., 1870.

Sievers, Joseph. "'Where Two or Three…': The Rabbinic Concept of Shekinah and Matthew 18:20." In *The Jewish Roots of Christian Liturgy*, edited by Eugene J. Fisher, 47-61. New York: Paulist Press, 1990.

Twelftree, Graham H. "Church." In *Dictionary of Jesus and the Gospels*, 2nd ed., 138-42. Downers Grove: InterVarsity, 2013.

Witherington, Ben. *Letters and Homilies for Jewish Christians: A Socio-Rhetorical Commentary on Hebrews, James and Jude*. Downers Grove, IL: IVP Academic, 2007.

CENTER FOR
CHRISTIAN STUDIES

The Center for Christian Studies (CCS) produces accessible articles and videos to help Christians and churches grow in faith.

- Videos & Live Instruction: Study Scripture and culturally relevant topics online or in person.
- Journal of Christian Studies: Explore biblical and theological topics of practical importance.
- Get Started Now: Contact us for a free, no-obligation chat to see how CCS can help your church members.

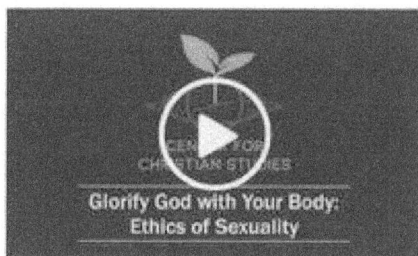

Glorify God with Your Body:
Ethics of Sexuality

ONLINE. IN PRINT. IN PERSON.

Web: www.christian-studies.org Email: info@christian-studies.org
Phone: 512.751.2728

REGNUM MEDIA

— for the Kingdom —

Regnum Media is the publishing imprint of the Center for Christian Studies. *Regnum* is the Latin word for "reign" or "rule," and our goal is to provide reliable, accessible scholarship for the good of the Kingdom.

Currently, we are introducing two new series of resources for adult Bible classes and personal study.

The **Biblia** Series is comprised of textual studies that take in-depth looks at different biblical books. Our first release, *The Search for Significance: A Study of Ecclesiastes,* by Luke Dockery, has been well received:

"Luke has done a masterful job of writing a curriculum that will help Bible class teachers introduce people to this life-changing wisdom. I can't wait to share it with the teachers in my congregation."

—**Wes McAdams,** Preaching Minister, the church of Christ on McDermott Road, Plano, Texas

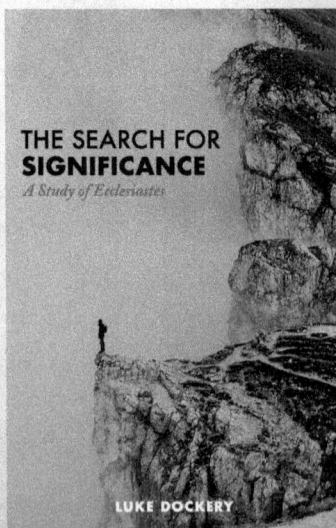

THE SEARCH FOR
SIGNIFICANCE
A Study of Ecclesiastes

LUKE DOCKERY

Three more books are slated for upcoming release:

- *Sharing His Suffering: A Study of Philippians,* by Kevin Burr

- *Following Jesus: A Study of Mark,* by Allen Black

- *Walking with Wisdom: A Study of Proverbs,* by Lance Hawley

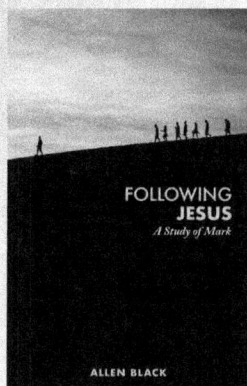

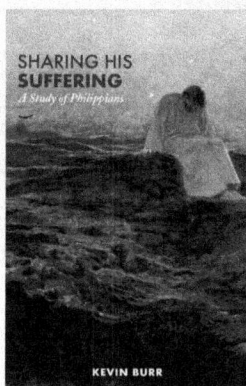

The **Doctrina** Series examines important doctrinal, ethical, and theological issues.

The first title in this series is *Transforming Encounters: Baptism, Assembly, and the Lord's Supper,* by John Mark Hicks.

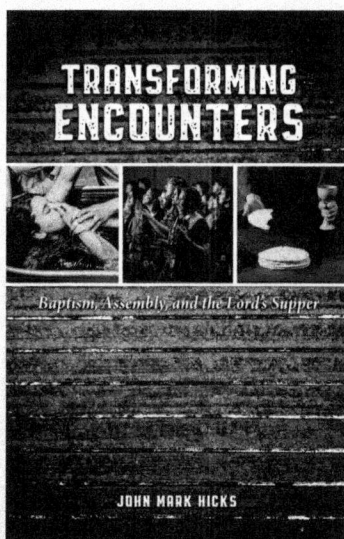